A Hole
in the
Market

the chief executive press

A HOLE IN THE MARKET

JANE BRYANT QUINN

whittle direct books

Charts: Barry T. Armstrong

The Chief Executive Press: Stephen Henson, Editor;
Ken Smith, Design Director; Evelyn Ellis, Art Director

Library of Congress Catalog Card Number: 94-060090
Quinn, Jane Bryant
A Hole in the Market
ISBN 1-879736-21-7
ISSN 1060-8923

the chief executive press

The Chief Executive Press presents original short books by distinguished authors on subjects of special importance to the topmost executives of the world's major businesses.

The series is edited and published by Whittle Books, a business unit of Whittle Communications L.P. Books appear several times a year, and the series reflects a broad spectrum of responsible opinions. In each book the opinions expressed are those of the author, not the publisher or the advertiser.

I welcome your comments on this ambitious endeavor.

William S. Rukeyser
Editor in Chief

For my father, F. Leonard Bryant,
former CEO of Hooker Chemical Corporation.
For my mother, Ada Laurie Bryant.
And for the long line behind them
and the long line ahead.

ACKNOWLEDGMENTS

My warmest thanks to Amy Eskind, who helped with the research for this book. I admire her for many things, not the least for her thorough, intelligent reporting and constant good cheer. And to Lynn Kane, for keeping everything in running order.

As I was walking up the stair
I met a man who wasn't there

—Hughes Mearns

CONTENTS

Chapter One

Slower Motion: Welcome to the Baby Bust

American business stands at the edge of a stunning demographic slide. The huge generation of young adults that powered the growth of the richest consumer society ever—the legendary baby-boomers—is slipping into middle age. Behind them lies the smallest generation of adults to appear in the U.S. since the 1950s and the first in our history to be smaller than the one before it.

The job of probing an unusual market change often falls to planning departments. But this time no CEO can afford to punt. Today's skewed demographics are diminishing demand not just in the United States but throughout the industrialized world, intensifying competition in all markets and upsetting tactics that have always worked before. You need to consider all the implications of this historic population melt, which will influence your decision-making for years.

At first pass, such a statement might sound overwrought. Nothing seems transforming about this new group of young adults, who hope for good jobs and aspire to their share of America's traditional bounty: comfortable homes, new cars, leisure time. They should be better-heeled than the boomers were (although they don't expect it now) and may be supported by more expansionary fiscal and monetary policies. That's a promising outlook. This book isn't part of the literature of American pessimism.

But due to the busters' diminished numbers, they cannot fill the boomers' shoes. Growth will stay modest for the rest of the decade, partly for the reasons usually cited (overcapacity, too much debt, global competition), but also because of this startling demographic drop. Too many companies are chasing too few customers. Spending gaps have opened up where formerly the money flowed.

Welcome to the baby bust, also known as Generation X. It represents a hole in the market where your most valuable customers lie. During the 1970s and much of the '80s, the number of young adults 25 to 34—the prime ages for buying and furnishing a first home—grew by 2 percent or more a year. Now their numbers are shrinking by more than 1 percent annually, a decline that will continue until after the turn of the century. Between 1994 and 2003, this age group will diminish by 12.5 percent. Had buster births just held their own, their cohort would have been stronger by 5.3 million souls. That's a lot of people who would have been buying cars, homes, life insurance, furniture, news magazines, sunglasses, and television sets. Had the busters *grown* by just 1 percent a year, they'd have added 9.3 million adults to the projected count and no one would be talking about Generation X.

But they didn't. The parents of the baby bust chose smaller families. Many couples opted not to reproduce at all. The consequent loss of young adults could take some $411 billion in direct purchasing power out of the economy between 1994 and 2003, according to the Commerce Department's Consumer Expenditure Survey and calculated in 1992 dollars. And that's only a fraction of the cost. Had that $411 billion been spent, it would have been leveraged into mortgage, auto, and consumer debt. So the loss to business runs to hundreds of billions more.

Some portion of this loss will be made up by boomers, who will be earning and spending more in their middle age. But that won't be enough to fill the gap. For many corporations, the simple pleasures of brute growth will not return for a decade or more. Businesses that carry on as usual face drops in sales to young adults averaging 12.5 percent between 1994 and 2003—and in a modern economy, one sector's decline affects others. Those companies that increase their sales in this changed world will have found new growth niches, bought or stolen customers from the competition, made technological breakthroughs, offered genuinely new or better services, or shopped successfully for business somewhere else around the globe.

International strategies, however, also carry demographic risks. Europe is coping with its own baby bust, as are Canada, Australia, New Zealand, and Japan. In North America and Western Europe alone, the number of 20- to 29-year-olds will decline by about 17 million during the 1990s, reducing demand for both domestically made and imported goods. This is far more than a marketing issue; it could be a matter of corporate survival. "Population helps govern the length and breadth of business' selling cycle," said Philip Caldwell, CEO of Ford from 1979 to 1985. "If the cycle gets shorter because the consumer buying power isn't there, it's hard for the weaker competitors to keep up." In the global market, only the less developed countries enjoy exploding populations of upwardly mobile young adults. Most of those regions show declining birthrates, but they're far from the snail's pace that challenges business in the U.S.

Magnifying America's baby bust is a marriage bust that started a generation ago. Boomer men and women married at later ages and at lower rates than their parents did, and so far the baby-busters have been even slower to wed. Faint signs do exist among younger busters that marriage is regaining popularity, but their pairings are still well below the rate at which the boomers said their vows. Because single households don't buy as many homes or spend as much money as married households do, the slow marriage rate among the busters exacerbates their already diminished demand.

Demographics aren't destiny, as any economist will be quick to tell you. Changes in rates of economic growth are driven by fiscal and monetary policies punctuated by the effects of trade, investment, legislation, recessions, and war. Tight money can strangle the purchasing impulse of large generations; easier money can draw extra spending from small ones. Expansive economic policies can be especially successful when the upcoming generation is small, according to demographer Richard A. Easterlin, professor of economics at the University of Southern California and author of *Birth and Fortune*, the seminal 1980 book on the link between demographics and living standards. The full-employment rate is lower than anyone suspects, he said, so the government can run a more accommodating monetary policy without igniting inflation.

Nevertheless, demographics remain the plate tectonics of the industrial economies. Shrinking markets give corporate policies a different spin than growing ones. You can work all you want at a sales or capital-investment plan, but it may come a cropper if you're not aware that the ground beneath your assumptions is moving.

Not long ago a businessman asked me how I could be so sure that the new adult generation would shrink. I replied that I couldn't tell him how many babies were going to be born because couples may change their attitudes toward family size. But if I know the number of 20-year-olds today and add a figure for immigration, I'll come pretty close to projecting the number of 25-year-olds five years from now. That isn't forecasting, that's *counting*. A surprising number of CEOs haven't made that count or haven't acted on what it implies, according to Ben J. Wattenberg, senior fellow at the American Enterprise Institute in Washington, D.C., who often speaks to corporations about the country's changing demographics. In his 1987 book *The Birth Dearth*, Wattenberg writes:

> I enjoy these talks. I learn a great deal about the workings of the American and global economy from people who are at the leading edge of business activity. But I have also learned that there is a great deal of ignorance about the demographic trends that will be shaping that business activity. Accordingly, I would underscore the idea that within this adjusting economy that must come about in the Nineties, there will be plenty of corporations caught with their trends down. Corporate America is not thinking far enough ahead, fast enough.

For examples of corporations caught with their trends down, you have only to study the late 1980s, when the baby bust was baked in the cake. There were empty desks in junior high schools. Many private colleges were accepting almost anyone who showed up with a check. You could readily see from the Census Bureau's population projections that by the mid-1990s growth would be only a memory in the blue-chip market of young adults.

And how was business preparing for the end of the baby-boomer gravy train? By *expanding* capacity worldwide, producing ever more cars, appliances, condominiums, airline seats, retail stores, and television sets. Some companies hadn't noticed that their target consumers had never been born. Others expected that boomer spending would compensate. But the increase in boomer buying power couldn't make up for the busters' loss—a critical point that many CEOs still fail to grasp.

The impact of the new demographics first hit home in the Bush administration. Suddenly boomers left the field and busters started straggling in. The historic changeover coincided with a national recession, so for a while one could cherish the dream that a strong household market would come bouncing back. But recession passed and the young-adult sector continued to shrink. Without necessarily understanding the population crash, many CEOs came to see that they were producing far more than anyone wanted to buy and at productivity rates too low to be competitive internationally. That's when corporate cost-cutting started in earnest—the layoffs and spinoffs, the downsizing and rightsizing, the radical changes in business structure that have raised profits despite slower sales.

No tenure is tougher for a CEO than one that straddles a seismic shift in America's social or economic substructure. Global competition is one of those make-or-break challenges. Generational contraction is another. A glance at the population charts in Chapter 3 shows that the downsizing isn't over yet. The number of young adults is shrinking. Real revenues will drop in the lines of business that serve them, even for companies that increase their market share.

Ironically, CEOs have been hearing for years about the bust. But the risk was presented chiefly as a shortage of workers. (Remember "Workforce: 2000," the joint government and private-sector study of labor trends, and all the hand-wringing that followed?) Hardly anyone saw the issue from the other side— that fewer workers meant fewer consumers, which meant lower sales and less need for high production. Because of the deep demographic drop, there turned out to be no labor shortage after all. The unanticipated shortage was of young people able and willing to shop.

In doing the research for this book, I found widespread denial that the bust would hurt corporate revenues or national economic growth. "We'll sell to the boomers," some executives said—not realizing that the boomers' increased incomes won't make up for buster income lost. "We'll export," said others—although many still have no handle on the complex rules of international competition. "We'll increase our market share," said yet others—a credible strategy for some but clearly not available to all. In any game of musical chairs, somebody is going to get bumped. My favorite denial is one I'll expand on in Chapter 4—that "young people don't spend a lot of money anyway." The truth is exactly the opposite. Young adults drive the economy more than any other group.

The baby bust alone hasn't caused the moderation in U.S. economic growth. Nor is it the sole reason for forecasting a tricky business climate for the remainder of the 1990s. But the bust is worsening the trend and making it tough for CEOs to come up with strategies that work.

To visualize the importance of the baby bust, think of today's economy as a long balloon. If you tromp on one end, the other bulges under an even tauter skin. Similarly, when sales to young families go down, the firms in that market push into other lines of business, stretching everyone's profits thin.

Slowed growth in personal spending also weakens business' traditional safety net. In any recession, consumer consumption never drops as far as the economy does, and sometimes it even rises. This helps companies slide by with a little less damage than they otherwise might have suffered. It also gives them some defense against their own mistakes. Errors aren't as painful when the money keeps rolling in. Lawsuits aren't as worrisome. But when the number of young adults falls, your cushion gets thinner, so recessions or mistakes take a deeper toll. In this way reduced buster spending affects the fortunes of all generations, young and old.

Some commentators on the baby bust see flattening population growth as the road to national decline: innovation will be stifled and profits snuffed in the absence of growth in America's fabled consumer markets. My research found most demographers doubting such apocalyptic views. Rightsizing an economy isn't fun. Layoffs and restructurings hurt. But countries don't require population booms to stimulate business communities. They simply need corporate leaders who see the fundamental trends and develop ways of profiting from them.

Even now corporations are squeezing higher profits from slower growth in revenues. They're finding new ways of raising workers' productivity so that real incomes can increase. Developing new products, services, and technologies, selling into underserved markets, lowering the break-even point, finding new markets overseas—all are raising returns on equity for CEOs who are looking at their American markets with a clear eye and demanding a recount. Above all, corporations are working off their crippling debt and overcapacity so that capital investment can pick up again. A lot of money has been made in eras of modest but steady growth.

As for the baby-busters themselves, they're likely to do better in life than anyone would predict today. You're going to love these kids for their stability, sense of responsibility, prudence, and social values. But they won't be the driving economic force that their forerunners were. Wherever your greater profit lies, it's not with the Youthquake anymore.

A number of the books in this excellent series have focused on, or at least touched on, *productivity*. How to attack it. How to increase it.

Similarly, several of our messages, sprinkled throughout the editorial contents of these books, have addressed how Citation business jets add value to their owning companies by enhancing management productivity.

A recent comprehensive study of 766 publicly held U.S. companies by one of the Big Six accounting firms sheds some important and conclusive light on the contributions to corporate success made by business aircraft. Those companies operating their own aircraft had greater gains in sales, earnings per share and productivity than their counterparts who do not fly business aircraft.

If you'd like a copy of this new 8-page report, or have any thoughts or questions on the subject of corporate productivity and the use of business aircraft, I'd be pleased to respond immediately.

Sincerely yours,

Russell W. Meyer, Jr.
Chairman and Chief Executive Officer
Cessna Aircraft Company

Cessna Aircraft Company · One Cessna Boulevard · Wichita, Kansas 67215 · 316/941-7400

Cessna
A Textron Company

Chapter Two

GOODBYE, BABY: THE DEATH OF YOUTH

As a growth market, youth is dead. It will not rise again during the tenure of most CEOs at work today. Anyone forecasting sales to this group from the experience of the past will almost surely be disappointed. What's more, growth in other demographic groups will not fully make up for the loss of youth. This dominating trend can harm not only companies that manufacture and sell consumer products and services, but also many of the businesses that stand behind them: agriculture, machinery, heavy industry.

In the past a CEO could pass for a genius just by hitching his or her business to the needs of young adults. Every year brought more twentysomethings into the market; every year they bought more of everything—housing, furniture, electric power, telephones, food, clothes, cars, entertainment, business equipment, office space, *everything*. This key group is now shrinking, even counting today's record-high net immigration. For the first time in the memory of most business leaders, twentysomethings need less and less. Consider the following Census Bureau projections:

- The early-twenties population will decline until 1998 and then turn up. But not until 2003 will this age group exceed its current size.
- America's foundation spenders, adults ages 25 to 34, will shrink in numbers until after the turn of the century. Then they

will slowly rebuild. But not until after 2015 will they again number as many as they do today. From 1994 to 1997 there will be a miniboom of 25- and 26-year olds, who are currently giving auto sales and household spending an encouraging kick. But starting in 1997 they too will go into retreat. Between 1994 and 2003 the young-adult market, including legal and illegal immigrants, will be roughly 5.3 million consumers short.

• A drop in young adults means a drop in the all-important household formations that launch the strongest spending drives. Net household formations are expected to run as low as 900,000 to one million annually during the 1990s, compared with 1.3 million in the '80s and 1.7 million in the '70s. Campbell Gibson, former demographic adviser to the Census Bureau, figures that the baby bust will cost the country around three million households over the decade.

• On the bright side, the teen population will rise. But teenagers' greater spending power (much of it through their parents) will be slight compared with the shrinkage in dollars held by young adults. Nor will the maturing boomer generation fill the buster gap by spending more as they move into higher jobs. Businesses keep targeting boomer buyers because that strategy has been successful for 30 years. But to the extent that spending growth is influenced by demographics, its rate is being governed today by the emerging buster group.

How did we lose so many young people? The story is woven from several strands. One goes back to the Depression and World War II. Families had fewer babies during those years, so it's hardly surprising that 20 to 30 years afterward there were relatively fewer women to reproduce. That's known as an echo effect. A dip in newborns in the 1930s meant a dip in the '50s, a dip in the '70s, and the dip being tracked in the '90s. The missing '70s newborns account for the current bust among young adults.

Another strand is the change in the status of women, which enabled them to enforce any preference for fewer children and turned a predictable dip in births into a bust. Several strategies presented themselves. Birth control became more effective in the mid-1960s with the introduction of the Pill. In 1973 the Supreme Court legalized abortion. More women chose not to marry or to delay childbearing. The increased migration of women into the labor force also favored smaller families. In addition, the divorce rate rose from 2.6 per thousand people in 1950 to 5.2 in 1980, putting thousands of women out of the baby business.

Yet another strand is the struggle boomers faced when trying to raise their standard of living. Income growth slowed as they crowded into employment offices and competed for jobs. Real estate prices rose as they sought out houses and apartments. Financially squeezed by a changing economy and unfavorable demographics, they married later and felt less able to support a clutch of kids. Boomer families in general earn 50 percent more, adjusted for inflation, than their parents did at similar ages, according to demographer Richard Easterlin's studies. But to satisfy their material aspirations, both spouses work and they decide to have fewer children.

Looked at historically, the boom was the aberration, not the bust. While it's no surprise that birthrates bulged in the years right after World War II, there's no obvious reason for fecundity to have had so long a run. From 1948 to 1964 the average number of births per woman of childbearing age—known as the total fertility rate—always topped 3.0, with a peak in 1957 of 3.7 births.

The most popular explanation for that extravagant urge to reproduce is the middle class's rise to affluence. Real incomes jumped in the 1950s, and houses and cars were relatively cheap. That made it easier for people to marry earlier, start families sooner, and add a third child to the basic American pair. Whatever the cause, the number of newborns topped four million during most of the boomer years.

The bust is bringing us back with a jolt to the long-term decline in fertility that has ruled the industrial world during most of this century. In 1900 the total fertility rate was about 3.5. In subsequent years it gently zigzagged down, then plunged during the Depression to a low of 2.1. At 2.1 births per woman, the native-born population replaces itself over the long run but doesn't increase. The unexpected baby boom rocketed fertility to levels even higher than those of 1900. Then came *le déluge*, which dropped rates well below those seen even during the Depression.

There are two ways of measuring the duration of the baby bust, both of interest to CEOs who are laying long-term strategic plans. Counting the number of infants born, the population descent began in 1965, hit bottom in 1973, and by 1980 had climbed back to its starting point. Since 1989, births have once again topped four million annually. Looked at this way, the newborn bust covers roughly the late 1960s to the late '70s and accounts exactly for the upcoming decade of missing young adults. As this attenuated generation makes its way through life, it will remain a constricting economic force. But soon after the century's turn, the baby boom's children—the baby boomlet—will start to grow up, promising more adult households and a resumption of population-driven growth.

It won't amount to anything close to the growth of the boomer years, however. That's because the total fertility rate—the other measure of the duration of the bust—has remained unusually low right through the early 1990s. Remembering that 2.1 births per woman is the native population's replacement rate, the rate in 1976 was just 1.74 and has hung below the break-even level ever since. In 1991 fertility stood at 2.07 births per woman, just a hair below the replacement rate. Since then, demographers believe, the rate has climbed a little bit. But compared with today's greatly expanded population base, four million babies aren't nearly the bonanza they were back in 1953. The effect of the fertility bust will linger for a decade or more.

A few more words need to be said about the baby boomlet, which will start coming into its own soon after the year 2000. Boomer women did indeed hustle to have children before their bodies rendered them genetically obsolete. But they came to it late and their hearts weren't in it. About 20 percent of boomer women will never marry, predicts Richard F. Hokenson, chief economist for the New York City brokerage firm Donaldson, Lufkin & Jenrette. Those who did (or will) marry, or who had babies anyway, kept their reproduction well below their generation's replacement rate. So although boomlet babies top the busters in number, they won't produce nearly as many households as their parents did.

Nevertheless, the boomlet is bigger than the bust, and that matters a lot. Its members will first make themselves felt as an important consumer force by the turn of the century. Around 2005, when they start to marry and form households, they'll be supporting a happier climate of accelerated economic growth.

Despite low birthrates, the total population continues to increase, although at a slower pace than it used to. Immigration at current levels (which the Census Bureau puts at 880,000 annually, including an estimate for illegal immigrants) equals a fertility rate of roughly 0.26 births, according to demographer Roger Avery of Brown University. That raises the effective count to an average of 2.34 births. So the U.S. is running above the long-term population-replacement rate and probably has since the late 1980s. Furthermore, the number of births is just about double the number of deaths, which makes current population trends seem more expansive than they really are. But when the Grim Reaper reaches the boomers, births and deaths will come more into balance and the flattened trend will become clear.

That's the big picture. Next, the nose count. Assuming you know the ages of the users of your products and services (or the users of your customers' products and services), the next chapter will show you the size of the markets you're fighting for.

·

RESEARCH INDICATES THAT OFTEN, THE ROAD TO SUCCESS ISN'T PAVED AT ALL.

A recent study by Arthur Andersen, a leading global accounting firm, showed that on average, the performance of companies purchasing and operating aircraft is far superior to those who do not. Of *Fortune* magazine's 50 companies with the highest total return to investors, 92% operate aircraft. Of *Business Week's* "Productivity Pacesetters," 80% own or operate business aircraft.

"No plane, no gain," is more than an advertising slogan for the business aviation industry. It is usually the simple truth.

THE SENSIBLE CITATIONS

Chapter Three

COUNTING NOSES: WHERE THE CUSTOMERS ARE

T o nihilists of numbers, population projections might
as well be pronounced by
astrologers as demographers—and I do concede that the skep-
tics have a point. You can count the number of women of childbearing age, but you can't know how many children they'll have
or how many immigrants will swell their ranks. As snapshots of
the future, 50-year forecasts are doomed to be wildly out of
focus.

Short-term forecasts, however, can be a powerful tool for businesses laying strategic plans. If you know the current number of
26-year-olds and the immigration rate, you'll have a good fix on
the number of 36-year-olds 10 years from now, which may make
a difference to your marketing or investment plans. In fact, a
growing understanding of the importance of population shifts
has led the Census Bureau to publish data more often about what
it thinks is going on. On its former haphazard publishing sched-
ule, you might have had to wait five years for fresh projections.
Now you can get them every other year.

For this book I've used the most recent projections, made in
October 1993, and stuck to a modest 10-year nose count. For
lagniappe, however, I've added the bureau's estimates for 2010
and 2015. Those figures can be useful too, and not just to astrologers.
Although the numbers won't be anywhere near right, they do

offer a reliable look at which age groups are going to shrink or swell.

These data obviously matter to companies that sell consumer products or services. But they're no less important to other economic sectors. Demand for forklifts is tied to housing starts just as demand for copiers and fax machines depends on the number of office workers. Whether directly or indirectly, everything from land development to public expenditures depends on individual consumers. Cities don't build schools or pave new roads unless enough people are going to use them.

Businesses use other demographic tools besides the growth or decline of the population by age. Changing incomes are closely tracked. More subtle but equally important are changes in the way people are arranging their lives. Take marital status. Some 90 percent of the people who marry eventually buy a home, but only 25 percent of singles do. Any change in the outlook for marriage rates—and the news here is that they just might be ticking up—changes the calculus for homebuilders and suppliers of home equipment.

And take household formations, which are America's money tree. Rising proportions of unmarried adults, men in particular, live in dependent relationships with parents or a roommate rather than setting up homes of their own. Dependent singles don't buy as much, or buy the same things, as independent singles or couples do. Rates of household formation, like marriage rates, may be turning up, but their numbers aren't anywhere near what they used to be.

With that as introduction, below is the nose count for the decade ahead. I've illustrated the Census Bureau's middle series, which builds on current trends. There are also higher and lower series, which bracket the plausible extremes.

Tots (0 to 4)

There's a dip in the number of children under 5 as baby-boomer women move beyond their childbearing years. Some forecasters think that the bust generation will be quicker to start families and have larger ones than the boomers did. But even if they're right, the busters' smaller numbers will hold down the production of tots. Early in the next century, however, the infant count will rise again, first because the baby-boomlet generation will start to reach childbearing age and second because of the rising proportion of African, Hispanic, and Asian Americans in

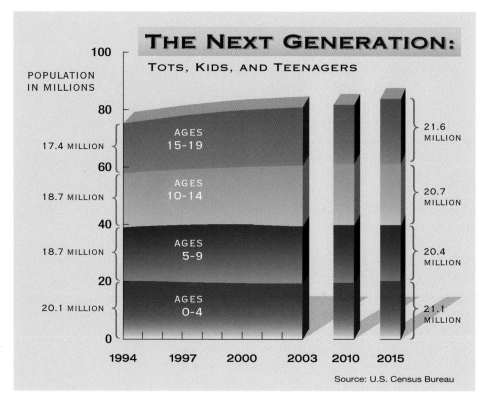

THE NEXT GENERATION:
TOTS, KIDS, AND TEENAGERS

POPULATION IN MILLIONS

100

80

60

40

20

0

17.4 MILLION — AGES 15-19

18.7 MILLION — AGES 10-14

18.7 MILLION — AGES 5-9

20.1 MILLION — AGES 0-4

21.6 MILLION

20.7 MILLION

20.4 MILLION

21.1 MILLION

1994   1997   2000   2003   2010   2015

Source: U.S. Census Bureau

The number of Americans 5 to 19 years old will increase in the decades ahead as the children of the baby boom march through their school years. But the number of youngsters below 5 will drop as boomer women move past their childbearing years. Not until well past the turn of the century will the infant count rise again.

the U.S. population, many of them immigrants. They tend to have larger families than whites, although their fertility rate is also on the decline.

Kids and Teenagers (5 to 19)

The kid market is swelling in the 1990s. Then it will drop off as the children of the baby bust (yet another small generation) enter elementary school. But the number of teenagers will increase steadily—up 15 percent in the next 10 years. These teens comprise the baby boomlet, not as overwhelming as the boom but large enough to get household spending moving again when they

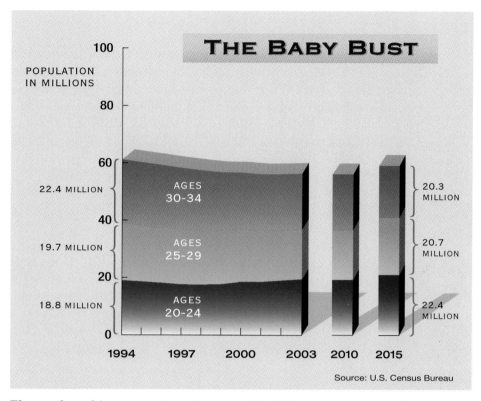

THE BABY BUST

POPULATION IN MILLIONS

100
80
60
40
20
0

22.4 MILLION { AGES 30-34

19.7 MILLION { AGES 25-29

18.8 MILLION { AGES 20-24

20.3 MILLION

20.7 MILLION

22.4 MILLION

1994   1997   2000   2003   2010   2015

Source: U.S. Census Bureau

The number of Americans 20 to 34 years old will decrease from 61 million in 1994 to 57 million by 2003—a 6.5 percent drop. The decline in 25- to 34-year-olds, those who historically power vital new spending for housing and related purchases, will mean a loss to business of at least $411 billion in direct revenues by 2003.

grow up. As young marrieds, they'll sway the early years of the 21st century. That's one of the reasons that so many companies now promote their brands to youth. The hope is that buying habits formed in the teen years will stick.

The Baby Bust (20 to 34)

Here's the missing generation (including some tail-end boomers) that will cost the economy so much. There's one bit of good news: we're now halfway through the crash among the fledgling adults (20 to 24). Their numbers will decline for just four more years— a further 8 percent loss, representing 1.5 million spenders. Then growth will pick up, although it will take until 2002 for this group to regain its current size.

The black hole in the market, however, is the next cohort up (ages 25 to 34)—all young adults of prime marrying and home-buying age. Except for a hump of 25- and 26-year-olds (discussed below), these busters will shrink in number until after the century turns. Between 1994 and 2003, business will lose 5.3 million dedicated materialists.

The Vietnam Hump (25 and 26)

Fathers weren't drafted for Vietnam duty. So in the late '60s, when the war, the protests, and the call-ups were at their worst, thousands of men took the family way out. If you want to know whether a man dodged the draft, don't ask whether he served in the National Guard; just ask him the age of his oldest kid. These protest progeny, now in their mid-twenties, make a short spike in what otherwise is a declining line in the number of new young adults.

For those among you who still doubt the link between population and business growth, this little spike is a nice test case. New car sales tend to track the number of 25-year-olds, and sales picked up smartly in 1993. These kids also are moving into apartments, buying furnishings, even getting married—coincidentally with a mild pickup in business. But their consumer spending spurt will peter out in 1997, when the decline in young adults returns to trend.

The Aging Boomers (35 to 49)

The bulk of the boomers are moving into their prime spending years. Over the next decade, this age group will grow by eight million, an increase of 14 percent. But huge as those numbers are, they can't overcome the bust effect. The extra boomer spending power will come to about $276 billion over the decade, figured in 1992 dollars, compared with a loss from the busters of $411 billion. That leaves the economy $135 billion short of direct consumer spending, with a much higher loss in spending that's supported by debt.

Furthermore, aging boomers are not consuming nearly as much as businesses expected. Some are raising their savings instead. Some lost high-paying jobs. Some saw the equity in their homes evaporate. Annual incremental consumer spending per person in the 45-to-54 age group plummeted to $231

THE MOMENT THAT CHANGED
THE ENTIRE FUTURE OF BUSINESS AVIATION.

When the wheels of the Citation X first lifted off the runway, corporate travel was changed forever. The fastest business jet in history had taken its maiden flight. And traveling at nearly the speed of sound had become a reality for business. A trip from L.A. to New York was reduced to less than 4 hours. New York to London shrank to 6½ hours.

For years, Citations have made jet speed a practical tool for excelling in business. Now, the Citation X makes it practically supersonic.

THE SENSIBLE CITATIONS

Cessna
A Textron Company

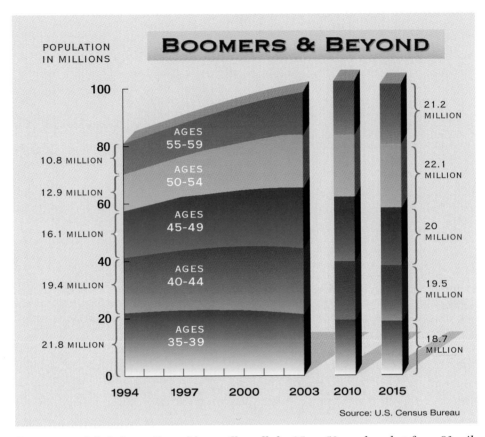

POPULATION
IN MILLIONS

BOOMERS & BEYOND

100

AGES
55-59

80

10.8 MILLION

AGES
50-54

12.9 MILLION

60

AGES
45-49

16.1 MILLION

40

AGES
40-44

19.4 MILLION

20

AGES
35-39

21.8 MILLION

0

1994   1997   2000   2003   2010   2015

21.2
MILLION

22.1
MILLION

20
MILLION

19.5
MILLION

18.7
MILLION

Source: U.S. Census Bureau

Boomers and their immediate elders will swell the 35-to-59 age bracket from 81 million to nearly 99 million by 2003, but their effect on the economy will begin to decrease as they hit late middle age and scale down their spending.

in 1992 from $1,417 in 1990. But whatever the size of their middle-aged consumption bulge, gather their dollars while you may. Early in the 21st century, the boomer generation's purchasing power will wane.

Prime Time (50 to 59)

Over the next decade, the fifties market will grow by 9.7 million—an eye-popping 41 percent. But this is a bifurcated group, dividing roughly at age 55. The younger fifties spend slightly more than they did at 40. But many of the older fifties are scaling down in early retirement. From this age on, falling consumption

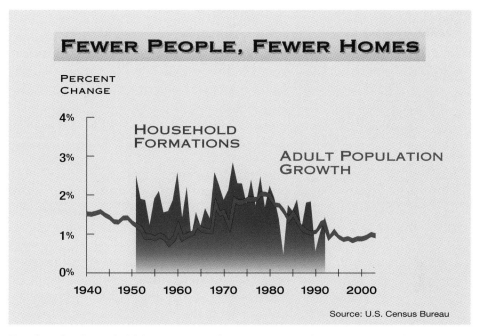

FEWER PEOPLE, FEWER HOMES

PERCENT CHANGE

HOUSEHOLD FORMATIONS

ADULT POPULATION GROWTH

Source: U.S. Census Bureau

For decades, household formations—the main engine of economic growth—outpaced even the rapid rise in the adult population. Now not only is the population trend weaker, but new households are barely keeping up with it.

acts as a drag on economic growth. That's another demographic point that many businesses don't recognize: the larger these low-spending age groups become relative to younger people, the slower the economy may advance.

The Late Show

All the remaining older age groups also are expanding. Between 1994 and 2003, business will gain 645,000 more buyers in their sixties (up 3.2 percent), 1.1 million more in their seventies (up 7.5 percent), and 2.4 million more who are 80 and older (up 30.6 percent). The older they get, the less they spend in most categories. They're a good travel market while their health holds out. But their biggest expenditures by far are on medical care.

Age-defined population breakdowns like those above are critical to business planning. But they aren't the story for the economy as a whole, where what matters is the change in the number of people who are earning and spending money. When their head count rises rapidly, companies can increase profits by expanding capacity. Today, however, their growth is low and probably going lower, even considering immigration. So America no longer needs as many new stores or production lines. In any demographic climate some CEOs will find domestic expansion profitable. For others, expansion awaits a more rapid rise in the living standard of the average American worker.

Overcapacity is even more serious in Japan and Europe, both of which face structural changes as well as a drop in young adults. Japan built an industrial machine to serve world markets that aren't expanding anymore. In Europe economic unification has driven businesses to consolidate. The world's explosive growth today lies in Asia and Latin America, whose young populations are earning more money and rapidly raising their standards of living. These regions don't offer big markets yet, but businesses are vying to invest there. As for Africa, it remains proof that population growth isn't enough. Because of inhospitable systems of government, most African countries remain off the economic map.

Any CEO is ahead of the game who takes the measure of the baby bust and how it affects the growth of his or her business. But in today's diverse markets, counting noses is only where wisdom begins. Age or income don't tell nearly as much as they used to about what people are likely to desire or own. We've split up into too many tribes, each with its own habits of life. Businesses need their own demographic research, based on how their customers live, how that affects their needs and tastes, and how their interests are evolving over time. Following are some of the stones that planners need to turn over:

Who's really earning what? Ingrained in America's psyche is the faith that earnings rise with age. That was so spectacularly true in the 1950s and '60s that we haven't been able to shake the idea, said economist Gary Shilling, president and CEO of A. Gary Shilling & Company, an investment advisory and economics consulting firm in Springfield, New Jersey. But you cannot count on it anymore. Median incomes flattened over the past 20 years, masking a sharp divergence of highs and lows. Pay is still jumping for proven top executives, managers, professionals, salespeople, and technicians. But middle managers "downsized" out of their offices may have settled for new jobs at pay cuts of 30 per-

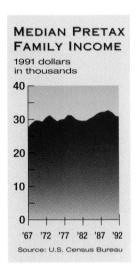

MEDIAN PRETAX FAMILY INCOME

1991 dollars
in thousands

America's standard of living grew strongly in the 1950s and most of the '60s. But for the past quarter-century, real incomes, and thus buying power, have hardly gained at all.

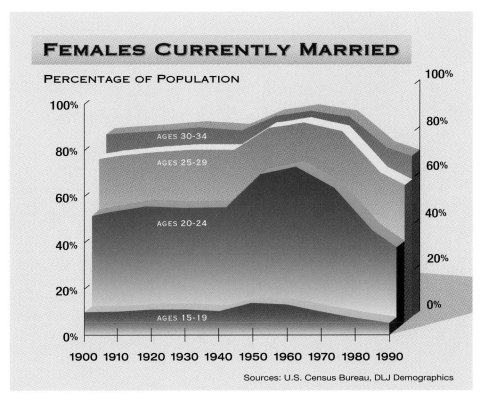

FEMALES CURRENTLY MARRIED

PERCENTAGE OF POPULATION

AGES 30-34
AGES 25-29
AGES 20-24
AGES 15-19

1900 1910 1920 1930 1940 1950 1960 1970 1980 1990

Sources: U.S. Census Bureau, DLJ Demographics

One reason for the low baby count: more women are staying single. The boom years for marriage were the 1940s and '50s; by around 1960, 60 percent of all females 15 to 34 were married. By 1994 the total had dropped to a mere 42 percent.

cent or more. Even when they keep their desks, their careers and real incomes may be topping out at an earlier age and lower salary than they expected. The number of well-paid blue-collar jobs also continues to decline. To avoid the carnage, many CEOs try to keep selling to the more affluent boomers. But that field is crowded. More opportunities may exist in selling to those squeezed down to a lower standard of living.

How many new nests? Forming a new household, whether as a renter or owner, is the single largest contribution most people will make to the economy in their lifetimes (see Chapter 5). In the early '90s, net new household formations declined to almost the fewest on record, partly due to the recession but largely because of the baby bust. Household formations have turned up a bit but

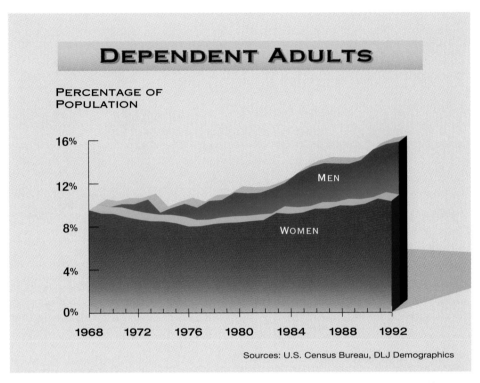

DEPENDENT ADULTS

PERCENTAGE OF
POPULATION

MEN

WOMEN

16%

12%

8%

4%

0%

1968   1972   1976   1980   1984   1988   1992

Sources: U.S. Census Bureau, DLJ Demographics

One reason for the shortfall in new households: many more adults, especially men, persist in (or return to) living with Mom and Dad or count on roommates for support. A lot of these adults have relatively high discretionary incomes, but they don't move the economy the way they would if they set up housekeeping on their own.

are still not robust. Slow growth in households comports with a forecast of continued low economic growth throughout this decade. Not until the boomlet fledges will that chart decisively turn up again.

Where did all the weddings go? The married often make different choices than the unmarried, not only in housing but also in the ways they spend their discretionary incomes. So how many of each are you dealing with? The parents of the boomers wed in historically high proportions. But both boomers and busters have married later and in proportions historically low. Marriage among the younger busters appears to be getting more popular (see Chapter 4), but even if that trend persists it will take many years to return to boomer levels. Of America's young adults,

30 to 40 percent are out of the marriage loop, hence highly idiosyncratic in their purchases, interests, and needs.

"I know, I know," you might say to yourself—but do you really? Richard Hokenson of DLJ Demographics said that executives tell him all the time, "We know about the new lifestyles." Then he sees them making business judgments based on assumptions from the 1960s, or even the 1940s, expecting the same growth in sales even though the world has changed. They fire their ad agencies, marketing VPs, or art directors for failing to make the world conform to CEO opinion. Said Hokenson, "They're killing the messenger when they ought to be trying harder to decipher the message."

How many dependent adults? Fewer marriages and higher divorce rates mean more households, which drive the sale of household goods. But these extra homes aren't filling the gap left by the bust. What's more, many of these singles, especially men, stay home with Mama or double up with roommates rather than strike out on their own. These dependent adults are better markets for discretionary spending—small luxuries—than one might guess from their incomes alone.

One final thought, this one on saving—another trend that companies need to track. As the boomers move through middle age, will they maintain their spending, or will they raise their savings instead? The busters already look like savers, the first young people since the Depression to be so fixed on financial security. But it's from debt and the liberal buying hand, not saving, that our great consumer economy arose.

SCHEDULE A BUSINESS MEETING
NEXT DOOR TO THE SOUND BARRIER.

Inside, it is an elegant conference room. Quiet. Abundantly spacious.
Beautifully appointed. With soft leather recliners, individual television
monitors, and a private dressing room.

Outside, it is slicing through the sky at more than 870 feet per second.
Mach .90. One-tenth of a point below the speed of sound.

The remarkable new Citation X. Reservations will be accepted soon
for demonstration flights in 1995. And they'll be going fast.

THE SENSIBLE CITATIONS

Cessna
A Textron Company

Chapter Four

THE LUCKY BUSTERS: WHY YOU WILL WISH THERE WERE MORE OF THEM

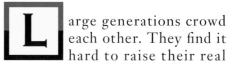arge generations crowd each other. They find it hard to raise their real wages or advance in their careers because of the hot competition for jobs. They fall into funks. All of their lives, they feel robbed.

Small generations, on the other hand, have the pleasure of being pursued. Their real wages rise as employers bid for their scarce services. They find themselves doing better than they ever expected, so optimism blooms. Because of their higher discretionary incomes, small generations offer much more vibrant consumer markets than their numbers suggest.

There you have the condensed, *Reader's Digest* version of the hypothesis Richard Easterlin put forth in *Birth and Fortune*. Unpublished research on the baby-busters by Diane J. Macunovich, professor of economics at Williams College in Williamstown, Massachusetts, confirms many of Easterlin's forecasts. "We're right at the turning point," Macunovich said, "right when interesting things start to happen."

CEOs need to study her findings, which are well ahead of anything in the public domain. They may change your view of the buster market—what busters will buy and how soon they'll buy it. Here are the blips that show on her charts:

• Although male workers in their early twenties aren't exactly flush, they're seeing a rise in their relative wages compared with those of middle-aged people. The previous young generation lost ground; young men's wage growth was stunted from roughly 1970 until 1985. Since then, however, pay rates of men in their early twenties have been rising faster than those of older workers. They didn't expect it; they may not even have noticed it yet. When they do, however, they're going to feel pretty good about it.

• Very young women are taking more part-time, traditionally female work such as typing and clerking. These dead-end jobs pay more than they used to now that there are fewer people to take them. They suit women who intend to stay home with their children rather than enter a career path.

• The plunge in marriage rates has been arrested among trailing busters ages 20 to 22. Since 1989, marriage rates have turned up for those who work full time or have some college education. That fits with the fact that young men are earning relatively more money. Young people in love tend to pair up as soon as they think they can support themselves.

• Couples are having babies sooner. Fertility has generally been rising among 20- to 24-year-old women since 1986. Even though some babies got postponed because of the 1990-91 recession, that dip will prove to be temporary, Macunovich says. Thanks to stronger business, the rising trend should resume in 1994. Women who have babies younger don't necessarily have more of them, but there are two reasons to believe larger families will result. First, early pregnancy helps some women avoid fertility problems, which might otherwise have prevented them from having children. And second, if couples continue to do well economically, some may decide to have one more child than they originally planned.

• There's a growing proportion of stay-at-home moms. Of women ages 20 to 24, only 69 percent entered the labor force in 1991, compared with a high of nearly 72 percent in 1987. This too supports the thesis that the earnings outlook is brightening for young males. Some mothers have worked reluctantly, from economic necessity rather than love of the job. If their families can live on a single paycheck, they'll opt to stay home and raise the kids. Emotions and ideology as well as economic change will drive this decision. Many of these busters grew up as latchkey children and hated having their mothers away. You'll still find plenty of young career moms and moms back at work when their children are older. But the incidence of twentysomething two-income couples has probably peaked.

At the moment, none of these trends applies to people 25 and up. A mix of trailing boomers and early busters, they're still averaging slender incomes, marrying later, and holding down their fertility rates. The median income for families with children headed by someone under 30 dropped 21 percent in real terms between 1973 and 1989 (a comparable peak year in the business cycle), reports Northeastern University's Center for Labor Market Studies. The losses were all to the less educated. Over those years, families headed by college graduates earned about 19 percent more (partly because of working wives), while those headed by people with only a high-school education earned 19 percent less. High-school dropouts suffered a 29 percent loss. The 1990-91 recession's effect on these families tells a similar story. Between 1989 and 1992, college graduates lost 4.3 percent of their incomes, high-school graduates 22.6 percent, and high-school dropouts 25.7 percent.

Real income losses among the young make it harder for them to set up their own homes. Among unmarried people 25 to 34 years old, 27 percent are living with their parents. Some are in school, unemployed, or divorced. But a healthy percentage of these boomerang kids have steady jobs that don't pay enough to support the standard of living they want, so they've borrowed a slice of their parents' prosperity while saving money to buy their own.

Forward-thinking CEOs, however, should treat these facts as out of date. The bulk of the busters coming up are nothing like the generation before them. They're Norman Rockwell as dreamed by Madonna: stoical kids with '50s values and '90s knowledge of the world. Their search for stability lies in their roots as children of chaotic times and, often, chaotic families. Compared with the young adults of the recent past, they'll get more education, earn more money and handle it more carefully, start households sooner, have babies younger, raise their children more conservatively, get fewer public benefits, and present a steadier face to society. They're entering the work force as purposefully as they passed through high school and college. Boomers call them materialists; busters call themselves realists. The boomers spent their twenties as post-adolescents; the busters spent their late teens as proto-adults.

Right now busters believe they won't do as well in life as the boomers did because the standard of living appears to be down. In a 1993 Roper poll, only 21 percent of the 18- to 29-year-olds rated their chance of achieving the "good life" as "very good"— the lowest percentage in 20 years.

FLIES LIKE A JET.
BUYS LIKE A TURBOPROP.

From the moment the first CitationJet took flight, the rules were changed forever. Cruising at 437 mph, the CitationJet is the first business jet that significantly outperforms ordinary turboprops at a guaranteed lower operating cost, *and* costs far less to purchase.

The technological advancements engineered into this extraordinary aircraft mean that even with a smaller price tag, the CitationJet has a great number of things the turboprop does not. Including a bright future.

THE SENSIBLE CITATIONS

Cessna
A Textron Company

What they don't realize is that the ground is slowly shifting. A wall of late boomers blocked the first busters when they moved into the labor market. But the younger busters are doing a bit better, as Macunovich's data show. Their shot at good jobs has not been as strong as it was for the small generation of the '50s—first, because busters both skilled and unskilled now compete with workers all over the world, and second, because companies have restructured their labor forces. But when the downsizing ends, full-time hiring will pick up again, and busters will be first in line. What's more, labor productivity is rising, thanks to the aging (hence more experienced) work force and business' increased investment in computers and other capital equipment. Over time this means that real pay will rise too. Life won't get brighter for the busters overnight. But given their meager expectations, their "life chances" will be better than they think.

Not only are relative wages rising for younger busters, their long-term wealth potential is also looking up. Thanks to low interest rates, national resources are leaking away from the older generations, who now earn less on savings, and streaming toward the younger generations, who now pay less on debt. The home ownership rate continues to shrink among those under 29. But as long as mortgage rates are low, more young people will be able to buy.

This good news runs counter to most of the dope you're getting on the busters. The fantasies written about Generation X have them hip-hopping cynically in their ripped jeans from here to oblivion. Ignore all that stuff. Expunge *grunge* from your memory bank. Busters will be pushing prams and putting their money in the bank.

So much for the good news. The bad news is that despite their better prospects they're still at least 5.3 million people short of where they'd be if the birth dip hadn't happened. Any business that sells to the busters, either directly or indirectly, will find fewer customers stepping up.

Why the busters matter so much

Young adults have a far greater impact on the economy than their incomes suggest. That's because *new* households add the most to growth. Those of us with established households represent the embedded base. When we buy a new house or car, we exchange it for one we have already. We may trade up to something more expensive, but we normally don't add a unit of demand.

A second car or home is a new unit of demand. So is buying a fifth suit to go with the four already in your closet.

But over the population as a whole, extra spending by the embedded base doesn't add up to much compared with the impact on the economy of newly minted young adults. New adults are pure start-ups. They earn less and spend less than their elders, but that's not the point. They have to buy virtually everything and are buying it *for the first time.* So they're adding new units of demand—for everything from big things like houses to small things like sugar and canned soup. Even a youngster who moves into a furnished apartment adds a significant new unit of housing demand. Because he exists, new apartments are built and the owner invests in the chairs and tables that set him up.

So what matters isn't the gross amount each person spends; it's the *additional* amount that wasn't spent before. As an example, take a college student who nets $3,000 from part-time work. When she graduates, she finds a full-time job netting $20,000 after taxes. One year later she's promoted to a $25,000 job. The year she starts to work full time, she puts an extra $17,000 into the economy. After her promotion, she has more to spend ($25,000) but only $5,000 of that represents additional money. So even though her salary is higher, its impact on the economy is less. The table below, based on the 1991 Consumer Expenditure Survey from the U.S. Department of Labor, shows how much extra money people in certain age groups put into the economy each year compared with the age group just behind.

Age group	Extra money spent annually
25 to 34	$12,296
35 to 44	$7,642
45 to 54	$231

The youngest group's economic impact is 61 percent stronger than that of its next elders and 520 percent stronger than that of families in middle age. Young people also carry more debt relative to their incomes than older people do, which raises the influence of their spending even more. So when the economy loses youth, it is losing a powerful source of growth.

The loss of start-up households is affecting the whole economy, not just the businesses targeted at young adults. Slowdowns in one sector are transmitted to others through job loss, wage change, and corporate restructuring. Older workers, downsized out, are bearing most of the burden of adjustment; younger workers just coming up will gradually find themselves more in demand. Profit levels will depend on how well businesses position themselves for the slow but steady years ahead.

Walter A. Dods Jr., chairman and CEO of the First Hawaiian Bank in Honolulu, put the problem in a nutshell. "Yes, the bust affects the bank's retail side, because we see a shrinking market out there," he said. "But strategically I also see it hurting the commercial side. My biggest loan customers are computer companies, shipping companies, and construction companies, and they need consumers to sell to. So no matter which road you go down, you arrive at the same point. If population growth isn't there, it has a dramatic effect on business."

This is America's second modern experience with a shrinkage in young adults. Between 1955 and 1964, while the number of people 15 to 35 grew, the upper tier of that generation—Americans 24 to 35—contracted by 0.85 percent a year on average. That decline wasn't as dramatic as the youth crash we face today, but it was enough to depress the growth rate for all adults (21 and over) to less than 1 percent annually. That was the lowest in this century so far, although likely to be matched in the late 1990s.

It is often hard to disentangle demographic and economic-policy effects, and the experience of 1955 to 1964 is no exception. President Dwight D. Eisenhower ran a conservative fiscal and monetary policy to knock back the big budget deficits built up during the Korean War. There were three budget surpluses during the 1950s—a tight rein that flattened profits, held down total growth, and produced three business recessions. Growth and spending didn't climb until the mid-'60s, when economic policies eased decisively.

But thanks to the generation effect, unemployment during those '50s recessions never rose higher than 7.5 percent, compared with 10.8 percent in the worst of the boomer recessions. Business investment had some good years, which helped productivity rise strongly, said Irwin Kellner, chief economist of the Chemical Banking Corporation in New York City. In the '50s and '60s real wages gained 4.7 percent annually, compared with just 2 percent in the '70s and '80s. Young workers' earnings drew closer to those of older workers, because companies had to pay higher wages to attract educated youth. As the '50s kids moved into the '60s, they started to win rapid promotions, which also pushed real incomes up. They rode the crest of the boomer wave coming up behind.

The '90s aren't the '50s, but there are some striking similarities. Antideficit policies have similarly been holding down growth, productivity is rising, relative wages for very young workers are on the rise after years of decline, and behind the bust comes the baby boomlet—a modest population crest for business to ride. The global economy does change the competitive rules, but the busters are better placed than they think.

One final point about these busters: they're far more prudent than young boomers were. I've learned this from being a guest on radio call-in shows. Over the past couple of years I've been getting a variant on the following question: "I'm 24 years old and have $15,000 in my 401(k) plan. How should I invest it? How much of it should be in stocks?" *Never* did I get such a question from a boomer. That generation was into spending money, not saving it.

Furthermore, I challenge you to ask any worker under 25 if he or she is saving money. If the worker has a steady job, the odds are that the answer will be yes. Besides the 401(k), there may be a savings account and little or no debt on the credit card.

The cautious temper of today's young adults derives from the disquieting world they've inherited. They see an economy twisted by unpayable debt, undependable employment, unending foreign competition, and a pitiless slowdown in the growth of America's standard of living. They're the generation born to pay for the excesses of the past, and they're preparing. Despite their youth, they're focused on the future: their jobs, debts, earnings, savings, investments, homes. As soon as you employ them, they will become the best-informed, most reliable customer base it has ever been your privilege to serve.

IN SELECTING THE WORLD CHAMPION MIDSIZE JET, THE JUDGES HAVE REACHED A SPLIT DECISION.

Many owners say the Citation VI is the perfect midsize business jet. No other aircraft offers more speed and more stand-up cabin space for less money. Many other owners say the Citation VII is the world's best midsize jet. It's just as spacious as the VI, but it's even more powerful, more versatile, and more technically advanced.

So, is the ideal midsize jet the Citation VI or the Citation VII? Judging by the popularity of the two, we'd say the answer is "yes."

THE SENSIBLE CITATIONS

Cessna
A Textron Company

Chapter Five

BIG-TICKET SPENDING: THE MYTH OF PENT-UP DEMAND

The argument for a strong pickup in growth depends in part on the theory of pent-up demand. After so many years of sluggish sales, the argument goes, consumers have mountains of unmet wants. As soon as they feel that their jobs are secure and their debt is under control, they'll unleash their credit cards. Then we'll see growth at the high average pace of the 1980s.

There are some problems with that view. Unemployment is already down from its 1992 peak of 7.7 percent, and it never reached the heights touched in the recession of the early 1980s. Outstanding consumer debt has declined as a portion of income. Mortgage rates sit near 20-year lows. Consumption has risen but didn't pour forth with its usual postrecession force. Instead of wondering how long it will take for business to get back to normal, consider the proposition that in most parts of the U.S. it already has.

Pent-up demand hasn't been the force that it normally is after a downturn. For one thing, buyers are taking longer to replace big-ticket items like washers, dryers, and cars. For another, many families have scaled back their spending to build savings instead. Underneath it all lies the bust. Any surge in demand by boomer buyers will be partly offset by reduced consumption from the young. This is a new phenomenon in America: the first economic recovery that's not supported by positive demographic trends.

Ask Marvin I. Moskowitz, president and CEO of Residential Services Corporation of America, how much thinking he does about demographic change and he'll say, "I think about it all the time." Residential Services owns, among other companies, the Prudential Home Mortgage Company, one of the two largest mortgage originators in the United States. Moskowitz's Team 2010 is preparing for a market very different from that of the past.

Prudential's analysts have concluded that the mortgage market is going to grow more slowly in the future than it did in the 1980s and early '90s. A smaller generation means fewer households coming up, hence fewer traditional mortgage loans. Slowed growth in real incomes among the young means that they'll be taking out relatively smaller loans than their parents did—at least until their incomes improve. Slowed growth in real estate values means fewer trade-ups, because it takes longer to build enough equity to buy a bigger house. These trends will constrict not only mortgage lending but all of the other industries related to home ownership. Even in a stronger economy, housing has passed its glory days as an American engine of growth.

Still, some corporations will grow despite a shrinking market. Moskowitz is crafting a three-part strategic response. First, he's reaching for markets that are poorly served. Roughly 65 percent of Americans own their homes; to grow in the '90s and after the turn of the century, lenders and builders will have to tap into the remaining 35 percent—most of them young. For builders that means putting up houses more economically. For lenders it means granting more mortgages to people who don't readily qualify today.

To attract and evaluate these new borrowers, Prudential is trying to reinvent its corporate culture. "We've been an upscale lender," Moskowitz says—a feasible stance in the flush 1980s but lacking potential in the downscale 1990s. In 1992 Prudential set out to increase its business in moderate-income areas and among nonwhites. "A team of volunteers from within the company stepped up and said, 'We want to do this,'" Moskowitz said.

The company is taking several tacks. It's identifying people in specific neighborhoods who might respond to a mortgage offer and bringing them in for counseling. It's searching for employee and alumni groups with large numbers of nonwhites, which could join its affinity programs for borrowing by phone. It's making more loans through mortgage brokers who do business in ethnic communities. In all of these markets, it's emphasizing loans with low down payments and less-traditional income qualifications—accepting an applicant with two recent job changes, for example. Moskowitz hopes to pick up business by offering these customers better terms than previous lenders have provided.

He is also making strenuous efforts to hire nonwhites and move them up the management curve. "Our company should look like our customers," Moskowitz said. "For example, we need Spanish- and Korean-speaking mortgage counselors if we expect to attract that business." Immigrants are an inviting target. In 1990 the foreign-born population stood at 7.9 percent, its highest level since 1940.

But Prudential can't move the mortgage mountain all by itself. Any significant expansion into nontraditional loans will require the agreement of those who invest in mortgage securities. Here's an example Moskowitz likes to give: Prudential was ready to lend $400,000 to a Korean whose down payment came from family members. But because he hadn't saved the money himself, the loan couldn't be sold on the secondary market. The loan—undoubtedly a good one—was turned down, depriving the borrower of a low-cost mortgage and Prudential of a customer. "We have to understand these underserved markets better and take more risks with disenfranchised people until their formal credit histories have been established," Moskowitz said. "If we don't bring them into the credit market, we're fighting a losing battle. Too many good loans are being turned down."

Moskowitz's second strategy is to streamline and automate the mortgage process, whose hidebound rules slow the market down. Lenders and investors snuffle through mounds of backup documentation for every $100,000 loan—in contrast to, say, the foreign-exchange markets, which move billions of dollars on a word. Mortgages could move quickly too if the industry were persuaded to change. Why not apply for a loan using your home computer? Why not present collateral on computer tape rather than in paper files? Why not make mortgage decisions in two or three days? "Successful companies ask themselves what is impossible, then make it possible," Moskowitz said. "If you don't, somebody else will."

Adopting new technologies is one of the keys to succeeding

in nontraditional mortgages. When loan costs are lower, a lender can afford to price more competitively. "If we improve the process, we'll all make more money because we'll be more efficient," Moskowitz said. "But we have to start now to give ourselves enough lead time to determine and absorb the technology."

Finally, Moskowitz sees tremendous consolidation in the industry. He's preparing for a system in which local lenders will be serviced by big regional or national mortgage originators. These originators won't need branch offices (he got rid of Prudential's years ago). They can do all their business by computer, fax, and phone. Prudential can grant a preliminary mortgage approval, long distance, in 40 minutes flat. Moskowitz boasted that one client "bought and closed on a house in Chicago in 15 days, without ever leaving Tokyo." That's the kind of service he thinks borrowers will migrate to.

"There's going to be a smaller pot of mortgages to divide," Moskowitz concluded, as well as a smaller pot of youthful consumer spending everywhere. "Those who can move more swiftly and flexibly and are the lowest-cost producers will absorb more of the business."

The importance of housing to the economy cannot be overstated. Every new home sets off a tidal wave of purchases: cement, lumber, shingles, electrical wire, pipe, plasterboard, furnaces, sinks, appliances, wallpaper, and windows. There's outdoor work: landscaping, driveways, pools. And financial connections: real estate brokers, mortgage lenders, title companies, lawyers. New homeowners need services: telephone, electricity, heating fuel, cable TV. They also add to public employment: schools, roads, garbage pickup, police protection.

All sales, including those of older homes, trigger new needs for furnishings: sofas, lamps, curtains, beds, rugs. And household staples: salt and sugar in the cupboards, dishwashing detergent under the sink. Older homes cry out for renovation: repainting, remodeling, relandscaping. One of every 10 jobs in America depends on the number of homes sold.

First-time buyers drive the new-housing market, even though they mostly buy older homes. The person who sold the house might decide to buy one that was newly built. If not, perhaps the person that *he* buys from will. Any net addition to demand will, somewhere in the system, wind up as a new home built and sold. According to the National Association of Home Builders, first-home buyers are generally 25 to 34 years old, and that's just the group now on the decline. Net new household formations, which averaged 1.3 million annually in the 1980s, declined to the one million range during the 1990-1991 recession, then edged back up. Even so, they're expected to be running at only 1.1 million late in the 1990s.

That's when the market will feel the full impact of the bust, as more of that cohort reaches traditional home-buying age. Already, decreased demand is apparent for apartments, condominiums, and mobile homes, which depend the most on people under 30, said economist Michael Carliner, staff vice-president of economics and housing policy for the homebuilders' association. Stand-alone starter houses will be the next to feel the pinch. In the 1980s demand for housing of all types ran at an average of 1.7 million units a year; since 1990 it has dropped to around 1.5 million; by the end of the decade, Carliner believes, growth will be in the 1.4 million range. The Vietnam hump will give the market a kick, but not a lasting one.

Why will housing keep growing even though the number of youthful households is on the decline? Five rising streams of demand will offset the buster gap: boomers who couldn't previously afford a home; immigrants whose primary dream is a home of their own; borrowers with modest incomes, who are getting a much closer look by lenders; affluent boomers seeking second homes; and boomers trading up to bigger and better primary homes. Trade-up buyers, however, don't add nearly as much to the economy as do first-timers, who represent a whole new unit of demand. Nor will trade-ups be as large a market as the boomer numbers suggest. In many parts of the country, home values are down 10 to 20 percent. Those unfortunate owners don't have the capital to buy something new. They'll be trapped in their homes for years.

At Los Angeles-based Kaufman & Broad Home Corporation, the largest homebuilder in California and third largest in revenues in the United States, first-time buyers remain the target market. But first-timers aren't young people anymore. "We used to look at them as married couples in their late twenties with 1.5 children," said CEO Bruce E. Karatz. "Today they're about 30 percent single, over half have no children, and their average age is 34 or 35." They're boomer buyers, arriving late. It took them seven extra years to accumulate money for a house, or to want one.

The buster generation is off Karatz's map. It's not large enough or married enough or moneyed enough to raise housing's roof. With young people out, Karatz is building principally for two substitute markets: immigrants and boomers. "We know quite a bit about Asian and Latin tastes, which affects the way we design our homes," Karatz said. For example, many Asians don't like stairs that rise straight from the front hall; they prefer them to curve toward the home's interior to aid the flow of positive energies. So in towns with a lot of Asians, he builds houses that have curving stairs.

Boomers, for their part, are approaching first homes with a greater feeling of permanence. "When first-timers were predominantly in their twenties, they planned to move up in four or five years," Karatz said. "They were willing to buy pure shelter that wasn't aesthetically charming because they didn't expect to live there long." Today's buyers, by contrast, expect to stay put for around 10 years. So they want homes with more traditional comforts—a porch, an attractive master bathroom, well-placed doors and windows, a cozier look.

But they're still first-timers, which means that they haven't much money to spend. To reach unhoused boomers—essential if his business was to grow—Karatz had to bring prices down. A Kaufman & Broad house probably costs around 20 percent less than its counterpart did a decade ago, he said. Much of the saving comes from lower land prices. But the company also cut materials' prices by setting up a national purchasing network—a change some of his divisions resisted. "They didn't like being confined to what cabinets or doors to buy, but for the most part we've proven that it's worth it," Karatz said. He's also shrinking home sizes by reducing the kitchen ("women aren't planning to spend a lot of time there"), scaling down the secondary bedrooms ("they're often used as home offices or workout rooms"), and including amenities such as vaulted ceilings and ceramic tile only in the family room, master bedroom, or master bath—rooms that the buyer cares about most.

Demographics aren't everything, however, even in the housing business. Karatz can afford to be cheery about the baby bust because so much of his competition got clobbered in the bust of the S&Ls. Billions of dollars drained out of housing finance, drying up the construction loans that smaller builders depend on. Their exit left more of the customers to the larger builders like Kaufman & Broad. The number of new homes built in

IN OUR QUEST TO BUILD
THE FINEST LIGHT JET IN THE WORLD,
WE CONFESS THAT WE CHEATED.

We had an unfair advantage when we made the Citation V *Ultra* the best all-round aircraft in its class. We began with what was *already* the world leader. Every year since the Citation V was introduced, it has dominated industry sales, routinely outselling its nearest competitor by nearly four to one.

Now, with greater payload, range, speed and advanced instrumentation, the *Ultra* pushes this pre-eminence to an entirely new level. At Cessna, we didn't ask ourselves, "Why tamper with success?" We said, "Why not."

THE SENSIBLE CITATIONS

Cessna
A Textron Company

California dropped 53 percent between 1986 and 1993; at the same time, Karatz's California business grew by 129 percent. Besides grabbing a larger market share at home, he's moving into new territory. In 1992 and 1993 Karatz started building in Nevada and Arizona.

To grow his business, Karatz turned to an older demographic group, which put him in competition with the builders already there. This proves the point that shrinking demand in one sector will affect other sectors that may imagine themselves immune. A business aimed at busters whose unit sales are going down, for example, might cut prices to hold market share. It might also try to broaden its base by crowding into boomer and senior markets. A fat and happy business aimed at boomers will suddenly face increased competition, which might force down its prices too.

You can see this phenomenon in home furnishings. The 28- to 46-year-old age group has always been furniture's fattest market, accounting for more than half of all purchases. These are people trading up, replacing the furniture of their youth. Their share of the market is going to grow, and everyone wants their business.

The stores that originally courted the young—Pier 1 Imports is a good example—have been introducing plusher lines to bring their original customers back for a second bite. But they're hanging on to their budget image; Pier 1's new lines are still cautiously priced. In response, the higher-price stores that depend on trade-up business—Ethan Allen, for one—are designing new lines at a price that looks good to a Pier 1 customer. So the fat boomer market has better choices everywhere, at a lower cost.

M. Farooq Kathwari, CEO of Ethan Allen, faced the challenge of converting a company that had made its name in Colonial design into one also offering lower-priced casual and contemporary styles. That involved changing the corporate culture. As so often happens when a business takes a new direction, he said, the decision to create new lines was "first rejected, then tolerated, then accepted. We involved all our people in the process." A contemporary line introduced in 1991 now accounts for 25 percent of Ethan Allen's business. And price is only the starting point in today's competitive markets, Kathwari said. Customers also want quality, service, and speedy delivery—no eight months' wait for a sofa they ordered.

Kathwari's other strategy for defending and enlarging Ethan Allen's share of the critical boomer market takes him, unexpectedly, back to the busters. True, there are fewer young buyers today. And true, they're not furniture's big market. But they're furniture's *first* market, and Kathwari is courting them aggressively. He hopes to catch buyers younger so they'll be more likely to consider Ethan Allen when they earn more money and start to trade up. "We want to turn customers into long-term clients," he said. Previously his target market was age 35 and up; now it's 25 and up.

Ironically, then, the smaller the youth market the more important it becomes. It's the point where the siphon starts.

A flat or declining pool of new home buyers carries echo challenges for every other housing-related business:

Real estate brokerage. Survival in low-growth neighborhoods requires raising or, at the very least, maintaining market share. One strategy evident today is volume marketing: brokers offer custom services to members of specific groups such as alumni associations or corporate employees. By early in the next century the edge will shift to technology: successful brokers will share in systems that let shoppers "walk through" houses on their home computers or cable TV. The industry will shrink as fewer brokers deliver services more efficiently.

Remodeling. As housing sales go, so goes remodeling. Much of the business comes from people who buy and renovate older homes. But most first-time buyers can't afford to renovate, while a whole class of boomers who might have traded up are now out of work or earning less. Even trade-ups, the largest renovation market, won't be as rich as builders might have thought a few years ago. That leaves senior citizens, a growth market often overlooked. They or their adult children will be commissioning renovations to help them stay longer in their homes.

Next question: Who will get this business? Many traditional remodelers are finding themselves locked in mortal struggle with small homebuilders who, lacking business, now bid on remodeling jobs.

Community services. Slow adult population growth means that tax collections won't rise as fast as they used to, assuming that Americans will remain allergic to paying higher rates. That will mean less money to pay public servants who, in some towns, are still getting higher annual raises than private business pays.

Autos are another major industry foxed by the dream of pent-up demand. In 1992, when sales finally touched bottom after a painful six-year slide, auto industry analyst John Casesa of the investment-banking firm Wertheim Schroder told *The Wall Street Journal*, "There's never been a case . . . where after a severe downturn the auto industry has had only a modest upturn. . . . This cycle won't be any different." Well, it was. The surging recovery never occurred. Pent-up demand did kick in in the summer of 1993, when interest rates fell, some automakers cut prices, and dealers aggressively marketed cheap leases. Still, auto sales ran at an uninspiring 14 million, two million below the industry's 1986 peak. Sales will eventually reach 16 million again, but that will be back to the starting line, not a takeoff.

Autos' modest upturn shows that boomers can't drive the economy by themselves. Those past cyclical snapbacks—so persuasive in charts of historical performance—all occurred in the context of growing numbers of young adults. Take away that growth and the upturn loses some of its thrust. Domestic makes gained market share last year, thanks to the price increase on Japanese cars, but overall sales just straggled ahead.

Not every demographic trend is poor. That hump of 25- and 26-year-olds, the Vietnam-protest progeny, is currently moving through the system, and this is a popular age for trading up from used cars to new ones. There's also strong growth among 35- to 44-year-olds, the age group (married, with children) that buys the largest percentage of new cars. If the youth market had just stayed level, auto sales would be soaring.

But it didn't. In 1992 around 16.6 million 20- to 24-year-olds held driver's licenses, according to the Federal Highway Administration, down from 19.4 million 10 years earlier. Reports from the Simmons Study of Media and Markets show the population of 18- to 29-year-olds down 14 percent between 1986 and 1992. That's 3.5 million missing souls. The number of new vehicles owned by this age group dropped 17 percent.

Auto dealers think that the poky economy explains the slow sales to young buyers, but they're only partly right. They're still missing the fact that part of their market wasn't born. The industry will face an even greater challenge when the boomers move out of their prime car-buying years and that all-important market, married couples with children, will rest on the busters' slenderer shoulders.

My conversations with auto executives turned up a broad belief that the population crash is going to be someone else's problem. Some think they have the right models for swiping the youth market from the competition; some think the issue is over-dramatized; some think this age group will buy its usual number of cars once its income starts to improve. One vice-president at Ford said the shrinkage in sales has had nothing to do with the baby bust. His "proof": small cars retain their traditional 20 percent share of the market. My rebuttal: the average age of small-car buyers has risen, so it's boomers, not busters, who are holding that end of the business steady. Many factors influence auto sales, but you don't lose more than three million young registered drivers without a long-term loss in sales.

The auto industry still presents a classic case of overcapacity, despite the plant closings of recent years. Worldwide, more cars are being produced for the American market than there are drivers—not only today but for many years into the future. The resulting ferocious competition has added to the array of lower-priced models, which helps raise the number of drivers who can afford to buy. The steady spread of leasing helps support the sale of costlier cars. But the industry still hasn't downsized enough. In late 1993, according to *Automotive News*, U.S. dealers were selling 28 imported and 15 domestic makes. "That's more choice than the market can absorb and that producers can present economically," said retired Ford CEO Philip Caldwell.

If domestic producers continue to pick up market share relative to imports, the greater adjustment will fall on Japan and other foreign manufacturers. Nevertheless, Caldwell believes that "all makers will shed models." The bread-and-butter part of the market, he predicts, will have fewer but higher-selling cars, because the capital cost of developing new models is now so large. "The challenge for CEOs," he said, "is to be more discriminating in placing bets on product development."

Although demography may be destiny for an entire industry, it may not be for individual firms. Some companies grow in leaner markets while others shrink. The game plan for U.S. automakers is to steal customers from the Japanese as well as each other—and, as General Motors sees it, busters can be the starting point.

Boomers remain the primary target. "By the year 2000, they're half of the market," said Vincent P. Barabba, formerly head of the Census Bureau and now in charge of GM's Business Decision Center. But boomers have an import bias. They switched to foreign cars at a time when domestics cost too much, used too much gas, and were often poorly made. And they largely remained faithful to imports even when the prices rose.

The way back to the boomers, Barabba thinks, is through the busters. "If we're going to be successful, we'd better get a higher percentage of them," he said. GM's strategy is to attract the busters with good prices and high quality. If more of them start driving GM cars, "the boomers will notice," Barabba said. "They'll say, 'GM must have made changes,' and our market share will go up." He thinks GM has a good shot with busters. "We've caught them with significantly improved products," he said, "especially in their end of the market. We think they're going to give us a good look." Still, he concedes, "with slowed population growth, the competition is incredible."

As a group, Barabba said, the busters refuse to be classified by any particular action or activity. They're more ethnically, economically, and psychologically diverse than the boomers. "Their needs are more complex than the way our divisions are organized," Barabba believes. "Manufacturing has to go from being function (a sporty car for fun, a staid car for church) to being more flexible." Okay, fine. But is anybody listening? "The auto industry has always had good information about its customers but hasn't always used it," Barabba conceded, adding that he believes "the guys at the top pay attention now."

If population growth won't raise demand sufficiently, maybe the industry can induce it by raising the velocity of sales. Cars, for example, used to be traded in every three years; now the average is almost eight years. "Nobody says it has to be that long," Philip Caldwell declared. "You might be able to pull the perimeter a little tighter"—the philosophy behind the explosion of two- and three-year auto leases.

To raise sales velocity also requires redefining the product. "Is the car strictly a commodity? If so, you don't have a lot of choices," said Caldwell. To encourage consumers to want a new car every two or three years, the industry has to persuade them that cars offer more than merely a means of getting around town. One strategy is planned technological obsolescence—a series of high-tech features or novel ways of using old designs that would cause consumers to desire new cars more often. High-tech features might include built-in telephones or electronic maps to help drivers find where they're going. For new uses of vehicles, consider the minivan. It used to be thought of as a truck, with BOB & SAM'S MEAT MARKET painted on the side. But sales jumped once it was repositioned as a chic vehicle for family use.

As for population change, Caldwell said, "it's one of the fundamentals a CEO should never lose sight of." Fortunately, he added, "it's also one of the easier factors to predict. You can see it down the road, so there's no excuse for allowing it to overtake you."

IF THERE WERE A CITATION FAMILY REUNION,
THE GROUP PHOTO WOULD LOOK LIKE THIS.

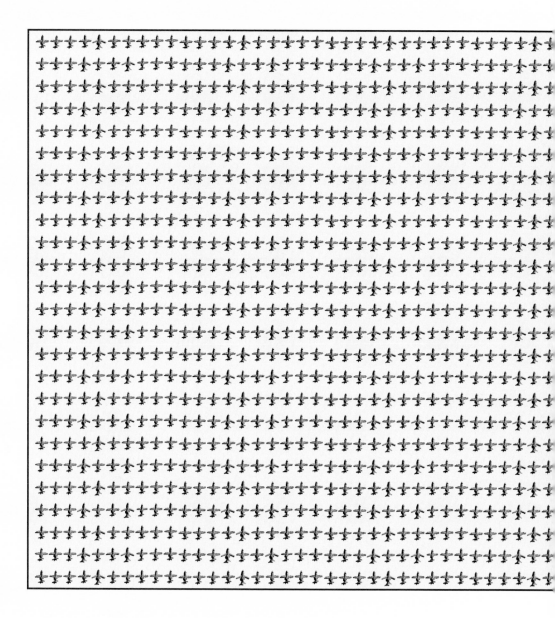

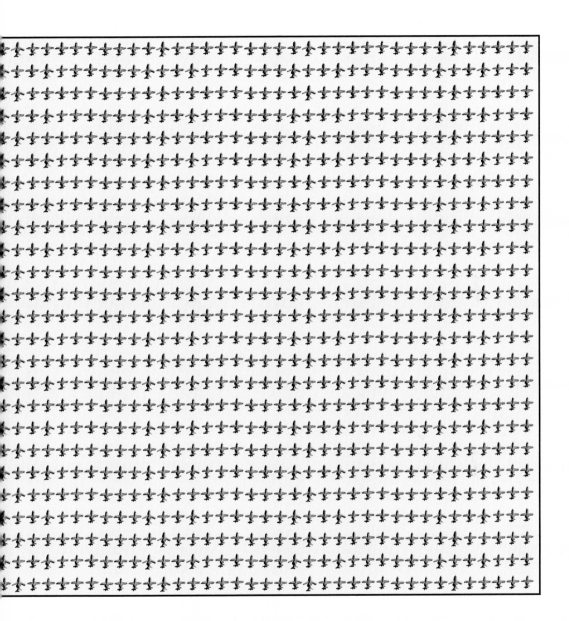

When the first Citation was delivered in 1972, its competitors had a big head start. They'd been selling in the same market for nearly a decade.

But buyers know a superior product when they see one. And they began buying Citations. Today, the worldwide Citation fleet has grown to 2,000 and counting. The Citation family has expanded to six models.

And something else keeps growing larger and larger, too. Citation's lead over those competitors who had that big head start.

THE SENSIBLE CITATIONS

Chapter Six

GROWTH OPTIONS: TRIALS AND ERRORS

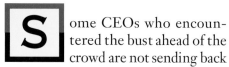

Some CEOs who encountered the bust ahead of the crowd are not sending back a lot of good news. Their best U.S. growth ideas often turned into holding actions. Smart strategic turns ran into a tangle of competition. The new-product advantage hasn't been lasting as long as it used to. As long as too many companies continue to chase the same customers with similar products, even the wiliest competitors will feel roughed up. Said one CEO of himself and his industry, "We're all sweating, but don't tell anyone I said that."

There are industries that have transcended the generational head count: business information services, generic drugs, fiber optics. And in any industry a superior company can dominate its market under almost any conditions. But in recent years, the standout successes have been fewer.

A slower-growing economy can be especially difficult for midsize to smaller firms. From the 1960s to the early 1980s, when new customers were abundant, smaller firms had a clear shot at niche markets while big firms broadcast their message to the masses. Both types of businesses grew steadily, thanks to the rising numbers of people in each target group. But when the adult population growth slackened, the industries defined by head count became mature, and fierce battles for market share ensued. Many creative smaller firms still manage to nibble the giants' lunch by offering sharper products, lower prices, or faster service. But more often the story reads in reverse. The giants, with their greater access to financing and distribution, move into niches, forcing small companies out. Said Harry G. Hohn, chairman and CEO of New York Life Insurance Company, success today requires that a company have "a certain critical mass."

"There's tremendous consolidation," said Carl Spielvogel, chairman and CEO of Backer Spielvogel Bates Worldwide Inc., one of the world's largest advertising agencies. "The power is shifting from the manufacturer to the large retailers, who market their own brands and tell the makers of other brands what size, shape, and color they want." That also changes the profit dynamic. A favorite Spielvogel story is that of the chairman of a $50 billion packaged-goods company who said, "We used to make 15 cents on the product and the supermarket made one cent. They're not going to be happy until it's the other way around."

In this tough but creative economic climate, almost all businesses have changed their ways of thinking. Some diversify; some concentrate on improving core products; some cut prices or add services; all slash costs. But those are good practices at any time. In my conversations with CEOs, I focused on their thoughts about how to dodge, or embrace, the effects of demographic change. Following are some of their ideas.

Shadow the boom

Some industries expect to prosper by clinging like barnacles to the boomers. Cosmetics, for one. "The older categories are an opportunity for us," said Jerry Levin, president and CEO of Revlon Inc. "Their numbers are growing and they use different products from younger consumers." In fact, Levin said, almost all of Revlon's new products over the next couple of years will be developed for boomer buyers. Like several of its competitors, Revlon has also hired older models to promote some of its brands—a significant change for a business franchised to sell youth. Said Levin, "The Lauren Hutton message is, 'You can look great at 50.'"

But other businesses that expected huge profits from the boom have been rebuffed. Take the life-insurance industry. In theory boomers should be buying new insurance products in large amounts—traditional behavior for people approaching middle age. But not this generation. Boomers aren't saving as much, or don't have dependents to protect, or are too broke to buy big insurance policies, or are putting their savings somewhere else.

Even if you're successful with boomers, that won't be enough, because boomers are a dying business. What will you do for an encore when this large generation starts spending less and the leaner buster generation reaches middle age?

Trust the bust

No CEO sloughs off the busters, who remain 40 million strong. Although fewer than the boomers, they're still this country's second-largest generation ever. What's more, consumers are hanging on to expensive purchases longer than they used to, so they're going to buy fewer of them over their lifetimes. That makes each purchase much more important. Any company that misses the busters in the first round may find itself knocked out in the second.

Chrysler is a company that aged with its present customers and lived to regret it. Having fought back from the very edge of viability, it is hoping to renew itself with youth. John B. Damoose, Chrysler's former vice-president of marketing, told me that the subcompact Neon, with its sporty styling and low price, is the automaker's "first real incursion into the buster market." Damoose shrugged off that age group's declining numbers, as well as the record tally of lower-cost models now being built. In his view, Chrysler has no choice. "A certain amount of brand loyalty persists as buyers move through the purchase cycle," Damoose told me. "The company has to be in this market or it won't ever get the baby busters into its cars."

On that he's right. Younger people display more brand loyalty than their elders, said David B. Wolfe, a principal of the consulting firm Wolfe Resources Group in Reston, Virginia. They're also influenced more by their peers. They like to own the same things that their friends do, so products that catch on with trend-setting youth will be bought by copycats down the line. Brand and product decisions that customers make in their early twenties may stay with them for a couple of decades. So even though it costs more per head to get buster business, companies can't afford not to secure their share.

Protect your tail

Alert CEOs have to focus on keeping the customers they have. Since the country is not producing new buyers at a rapid rate, everyone is trying harder to poach business from everyone else.

For example, credit-card issuers like AT&T have paid borrowers to switch their balances from their bank cards to the AT&T card. Because growth in the food industry depends on population trends, the Sara Lee Corporation's chairman and CEO, John H. Bryan, diversified into packaged apparel like hosiery and sweatsuits and is shooting down competitors both here and abroad.

The need to protect your customer base explains all the loyalty-building programs, of which frequent flier is the model, said Jerome W. Pickholz, chairman and CEO of Ogilvy & Mather Direct, specialists in direct marketing. That's why food companies mail their customers newsletters that contain recipes and why cosmetics firms send beauty information to people who have bought their products before. "Price and quality matter, but it takes more than that to build loyalty today," Pickholz said. "It takes a level of service that tells customers that you know who they are and you recognize their needs."

In the advertising business, that means offering clients a broader range of services. "They're all reengineering their work forces to get more productivity from fewer people," Pickholz said. "We have to provide more specialized skills to fill in the gaps and still keep the costs down—that's essential in a stagnant market." Clients also seek to target their audiences more precisely, through cable shows, mail, shopping channels, interactive computer networks, stand-alone stores—anything that lessens the distance between the customer and the product.

Loyalty programs and superior service are especially critical to retaining boomer business, because older customers are choosier, David Wolfe said. They're less swayed than the young by a brand name and more aware of total value. By *value* Wolfe means service and durability as well as price. This base of aging, more discriminating consumers is one of the reasons for the decline in brand loyalty today. "You can see this when you watch shoppers," Carl Spielvogel said. "In supermarkets, people read the ingredients on the back of the package carefully. In auto showrooms, they go through the catalog slowly" and ask questions about the car. With customers like these, there's no kidding around.

Go younger

If the young develop a crush on brands, how early can you capture them? Some CEOs are targeting buyers as early as grade school. There are kids' clubs created to sell brand-name products, teaching materials that mention product names, ads in special newspapers that are distributed in classrooms, diet brochures for teens in supermarkets. Capturing the kid may mean capturing the parent too.

CEOs may even buy a business or start a new line of products specifically to get their names before the young. Yogurt makers, for one, are developing stronger, sweeter flavors for kids in hopes of retaining them as customers when they grow up. Today's teens represent a long-term demographic opportunity. They're the famous baby boomlet—the well-loved, well-equipped children of the doting boomers. For the next 10 to 15 years, their numbers and spending power will swell. They're America's next big young-adult market that will ultimately help push business forward again.

Go older

The 60-plus crowd used to be magisterially ignored. They were thought to have no money, no mobility, and no *joie de vivre*. That's no longer true, if it ever was. They're already the travel industry's darlings, and other industries should be romancing them too. "The prime market used to be 18 to 45, but no longer," Carl Spielvogel said. It's rolling out at the older end.

Bruce Karatz of Kaufman & Broad foresees a housing market adapted to the old. "You might be able to add something to the design of a house that would help older people while not detracting from the home's appeal to the young," he said—things like appliances with larger and more readable lettering, knobs that are easier to operate, bathrooms a couple of inches wider to accommodate a walker, and a bedroom and bath on the first floor.

From this point of view, the elderly aren't a narrow market. Many products that suit them will suit the general public too—knives with wider handles, big-number telephones and clocks, box tops you can open without a power saw. Instead of projecting from young adults up, CEOs can successfully project from old people down.

Health care is an obvious industry where aging boomers will make the market and the baby bust hardly matters. Jane Hirsh, chairman, president, and CEO of Copley Pharmaceutical Inc., banked an estimated $148 million last year when she sold 51 percent of her generic drug company to Hoechst Celanese Corporation to get the resources to expand. At New York Life, CEO Harry Hohn has enlarged his company's stake in managed care and is looking at nursing homes. "We think the market dynamics are changing here," he said. "People are starting to think about

HOW MANY TECHNICIANS DOES IT TAKE TO CHANGE A LIGHT BULB?

With our Integrated Design program, every concept our engineers develop is evaluated not simply on how it enhances performance, but on how it affects all other aspects of the aircraft. Things like comfort, safety, efficient use of space, and serviceability all go into the equation.

Without this kind of planning, something as simple as changing a fuse or even a light bulb could easily become a complex chore for the aircraft owner. But Integrated Design ensures that no one designing *or operating* a Citation is ever left in the dark.

THE SENSIBLE CITATIONS

Cessna
A Textron Company

nursing homes as something better than a last resort." In the mid-1980s New York Life considered a joint venture with a major hotel chain to combine health care facilities with managed adult communities. "We decided the time wasn't right then," he said. "But attitudes are different today. The right time may be rapidly approaching." Such a pairing would match giant with giant—the overriding business dynamic as America plunges toward the end of the 20th century.

Boomers and seniors also dominate the money-management market, an industry swarming with new players. Banks, insurance companies, nonbank financial institutions like General Electric Capital Corporation, stockbrokerages, and pension funds all are battling for the business. To survive in the 21st century, said Charles L. Gummer, president of Comerica Bank (Texas), a bank will have to sell annuities and mutual funds. Otherwise its customers will do their investing at other banks and might give those banks their loan and deposit business too. "Eventually," he adds, "a bank will have to have its own branded mutual funds if it is to maintain its long-term profitability."

Drop down

Wal-Mart's Sam Walton saw it early. As the gap widened between rich and poor, as the number of lower-income households grew, as young people saw their incomes drop, as single motherhood increased, as layoffs persisted, the downscale market enlarged phenomenally. In general, anyone earning more than $10,000 has at least some discretionary income, as Cheryl Russell and Margaret Ambry report in their 1993 book *The Official Guide to American Incomes*. Serving the poor, the near-poor, and the white-collar "new poor"—as well as the price-conscious middle class—can be just as profitable as jousting with all of the firms that pursue the rich. Some banks, for example, are looking into owning check-cashing services in low-income neighborhoods. Factory-discount outlets are moving to the suburbs to compete with malls.

To maintain their low-price reputations, Wal-Mart, Price Club, Costco, Target, and Home Depot exert a powerful control over their wholesale cost of goods. According to Carl Spielvogel, one company that makes an oil additive for automobiles was forced to give Wal-Mart such a big discount that a gray market grew up. Entrepreneurs cleaned off Wal-Mart's shelves and resold the product at a profit.

It was a couple of years ago that mass merchants attracted the attention of Revlon's Jerry Levin. Watching the upscale department stores struggle, he decided he'd do better by selling some premium lines through drugstores, Wal-Marts, and Kmarts instead. Now he's a market leader in both upscale and downscale stores. "The younger customer saw the value early," Levin explained. "She said, 'Why should I buy a lipstick for $20 at a major department store when I can buy a perfectly good one in a drugstore for $6?'"

Change colors

CEOs are picking up market share by addressing the members of various black, Hispanic, and Asian communities. The discount brokerage firm Charles Schwab, for example, has opened an Asia Pacific Center in San Francisco primarily for Chinese Americans and a Latin America Center in Miami, both with 800 telephone lines. Kentucky Fried Chicken added African kente cloth to employees' uniforms in 300 of its stores that are patronized largely by blacks.

Advertising to ethnic markets is yesterday's news. Tomorrow's successful CEOs will own a piece of the enormous buying power that nonwhite consumers wield. For predominantly white companies, that means creating products skewed to minorities or buying the companies whose products minorities use already. A start-up comes from Gerber Products, whose baby-food business faces yet another bust at the end of the century. The company's three-year-old Tropical line of foods features flavors and ingredients likely to attract Hispanics, who, early in the next century, will overtake African Americans as the U.S.'s largest minority group. A striking example of one company's buying another came in 1993, when Ivax Corporation bought Johnson Products Company, a pioneer in hair-care products for African Americans. For Johnson's chairman and CEO, Joan B. Johnson, the sale was a way of energizing her company's growth. For Ivax, it offered a stronger hold on a growing niche market (the company also owns Flori Roberts Inc., maker of cosmetics for black women). "This purchase said that black businesses have come of age," said Earl G. Graves, president of *Black Enterprise* magazine and of the bottling company Pepsi-Cola of Washington, D.C. "People can look at a business skewed to the black consumer and say, 'It has high enough profits, a viable market, and it's an opportunity for our company. I'm going to make an investment.'"

In cosmetics all the major firms are now bidding for the darker-skinned and ethnic markets by creating new lines or by adding new shades to existing lines. "African American women like products designed specifically for them," Jerry Levin said. "Hispanic women prefer regular products in their skin shades but marketed in Spanish or in commercials that otherwise recognize their cultural differences." He believes that Asian marketing will follow the Hispanic pattern. In 1994 Revlon rolled out its first commercial featuring an Asian model.

Because of their potential for worldwide sales, products aimed at darker-skinned and ethnic buyers also serve a global strategy. "China, India, the Latin American markets, they're all very exciting, with an abundance of opportunities," Levin said. At home such products can help capture more of the buster buyers. A growing proportion of this generation is nonwhite or Hispanic white, in part because of the youthful immigrants pouring into the United States. By 2010, when the busters are 30 to 39, nearly 19 percent of them will be foreign-born (Asian and Latin American, especially), compared with only 5 percent of the boomers of that age today.

This thriving portion of the market still hasn't been decoded by most predominantly white corporations, other than those selling sneakers and teenage fashions. But unlike most of their predecessors, CEOs today know they have to learn. It helps when they get the right executives to advise them. I give a lot of speeches to business groups, and I don't see nearly enough skin colors in the audience for companies that expect to preside over the 21st century.

For firms that are minority-oriented and -led, the fat part of the business is coming up—from immigrants and from the rising purchasing power of their American customers. So they're not much harmed by the fertility decline, which has occurred among minorities too. "We continue to make economic gains, our enterprises are going mainstream, and businesses see the value of the black consumer," Earl Graves said. Franchisers who once ignored this market now seek out black business people. The minority business' challenge, in fact, is the mainstream giant that, increasingly, will tread on its turf. "Nothing is forever," Graves said. "There's more competition for the black consumer, and our businesses have to face it. My premise is that you have to be prepared to do business on the '100 percent corner,' which is a community's dead center: Main Street, U.S.A."

Go abroad

"I don't know any CEOs who can escape looking at their businesses globally," said former Ford CEO Philip Caldwell. "Even if they're not selling abroad, they're being impacted by international competitors." And indeed, almost every CEO I spoke with is selling, manufacturing, or investing abroad. The growth they're anticipating today comes not so much from the industrialized world, including Europe and Japan, as from the energetic developing countries, where young-adult populations are exploding and real wages are on the rise. Jerome Pickholz of Ogilvy & Mather Direct, which has offices all over the world, said that the United States accounted for less than half of his business last year, with Europe second—but the Far East was the fastest-growing segment. Latin America "won't move the needle this year," he said, "but will be more important in two or three years."

Thomas B. Wheeler, president and CEO of Massachusetts Mutual Life Insurance Company, said the fastest-growing insurance markets are also in the Pacific region as well as in South America. "Very few U.S. insurance companies have gone abroad so far," he said, "but in five to 10 years this industry is going to be global." Wheeler has a toe in the British health-insurance business, selling to affluent buyers who want to supplement their state-supplied coverage. "But unless we get something more launched," he said, "we're going to miss a very significant market."

Sounding a warning is Walter Dods of First Hawaiian Bank. "You have to go out of your market for growth," he said, "but you don't know the area as well and it's harder to manage the business long distance. So you're exposing the company and the shareholders to greater risk."

Cruise cyberspace

"The rate of change in technology is off the wall," said Harry Hohn. "CEOs need technological expertise or they won't know where to turn." In fact, I'd add that CEOs whose minds don't reach the datastream should retool or retire for the good of the companies they lead. Already some 75 to 80 percent of New York Life's policies are underwritten and issued electronically. In the future almost anyone will be able to call an 800 number worldwide to get information, buy policies, make loans, and switch policy investments. "We're developing that capability now on a regional basis," Hohn said. As I write, New York Life's Dallas

Service Center has its 800 number up and running. By the time this book reaches you, Cleveland will also be on line.

Money management too is a highly computerized business—calling, for example, for systems that read prospectuses on disk and analyze what a bond will do under various interest and market scenarios. "You have to have that at your fingertips to compete," Hohn said. "We have computers in our pension area that can take a prospectus on a floppy disk, analyze the data, and in five or 10 minutes project what the cash flows are going to be. We know what the income stream will be like in the 14th, 17th, or 22nd year, while other pension managers are still reading the prospectus."

These systems don't come cheap. But no one will be able to play with the big guys who can't afford to upgrade his or her company's technological base. Consider Walgreen. During 1993 its new high-tech Strategic Inventory Management System saved $80 million at three distribution centers by tracking inventory shrinkage and holding down costs, giving the company a tremendous advantage over slower-moving competitors. Walgreen expects to save $200 million by the end of 1994, when the whole system is up and running.

Much technology remains in waiting, while the telephone and cable companies sort out who controls the wires and information services going into homes. But every major communications company is at least experimenting with CD-ROM and interactive connections, the next major media in an information-driven world. In a first-ever experiment, masterminded by Ogilvy & Mather Direct, ads from 10 companies were put on a compact disc and bound into *Forbes* magazine. The Seagram's message included a murder mystery that, if solved, printed out a $5 discount coupon for a bottle of Glenlivet; the Jaguar message let consumers call up a car's specs and financing options. Magazine CEOs should consider that disc a wake-up call. Even display advertising can be torn from your pages and entered into the datastream.

Roll the dice

More money should be rolling into research. A fresh idea, not just modifications of stale old ones, can spring a company out of the population trap. Take the makers of contraceptive pills. Young women are the primary target. Although marketers have had some success in raising their use among women over 40, the number of new prescriptions has been dropping off. Enter CEOs

CESSNA HAS INVESTED A QUARTER-BILLION DOLLARS TO KEEP CITATION OPERATORS IN THEIR PLACE.

A Citation's place is in the sky. That's why every Citation is supported by the largest single-product network of any business jet in the world. Today, eight Cessna-owned Citation Service Centers are dedicated entirely to Citations. And Authorized Citation Service Centers are located around the globe. It's a quarter-billion-dollar investment.

We figure the more we spend on the Citation service network, the less time Citation owners will spend on the ground.

THE SENSIBLE CITATIONS

allocating cash. The future will lie with the company whose scientific breakthrough creates a new form of contraception so appealing that the Pill will molder in the bottom drawer.

Corporations of many other stripes are hunting for technological exits. Joseph H. Williams, former chairman and CEO of the Williams Companies, holder of gas pipelines and telecommunications, has said it best: "The only way you really excel in a capital-intensive business is to invest your way into the future." The discoveries made under such CEOs will lay the foundations for the unimaginable new industries of the 21st century.

Go lean

"In a stagnant market, I have to be better, smarter, and more efficient than the competition," Jerome Pickholz said. "That could mean a lower margin unless I can work on the cost side of the equation." Walter Dods identifies this decade's survivors as "low-cost producers, innovators, efficient providers of services doing the job better than anybody else." But that may only preserve your market share or raise it incrementally, Dods added. By itself it won't work as a strategy for growth.

Sell out

The classic shrinking industry is life insurance, which started to implode as far back as the boom's waning days. Sales of new policies declined during most of the 1980s due to lifestyle changes that lowered the need for insurance protection—things like two-income families, rising numbers of singles, and fewer families with children. Then came the bust, presenting insurers with the prospect of fewer young families, period. The number of life- and health-insurance companies hit a high-water mark in 1988 and since then has declined.

"I'm surprised there haven't been more mergers," said Tom Wheeler of Mass Mutual. "There are too many companies with too little market share." What impedes consolidation? "The ego of the CEO," Wheeler said. "They tend to say, 'Not on my watch; we can make it,' even though merging would create value for policyholders." But their watch may be shorter than they think. "The volume of sales helps determine unit cost, and it takes a broad customer base to compete effectively," Harry Hohn said. Of some 2,000 life insurance companies today, the number able to compete could drop to 500 by the end of the decade, he added.

Seeking a growth path, some insurers have headed for the market's affluent end. "The amount of business we're doing with people over 65, and the size of their policies, is huge," Wheeler said. Others have redefined their businesses, focusing on annuities and the investment-management business. Yet others settle in the niches, like credit life.

Which companies will make it? Looks are deceiving, said Michael Albanese, assistant vice-president of the venerable insurance rater A.M. Best in Oldwick, New Jersey. A life insurer can seem financially strong, thanks to healthy renewal premiums. But it's doomed if it can't find a strategy for adding substantial new business to the books. "With today's demographics," said Albanese, "you can't just work harder and be all right."

For another industry in that same bind, consider beer, whose primary market by far is youth. As a population ages, its consumption of beer gradually declines. The larger brewers, like Anheuser-Busch, have snatched market share from second-tier firms. Brand names are proliferating. Competitors scour the niche markets, such as women, who don't drink much beer; older people, who might tumble for nonalcoholic brews; and the hardest-drinking young, who buy high-powered malts. But at some point, said beer-industry consultant R. S. Weinberg, the cost of pursuing market share will become prohibitive for some firms. They'll sell out. Or they'll maximize short-term profits, invest in something else, and wait for the baby boomlet to save them.

One point I can't emphasize enough is that the baby bust tows a long tail. In their twenties busters will annoy some industries, and in their thirties and forties they'll annoy others. Take the advertising business. The amount of money spent on advertising, relative to economic growth, has depended on the growth rate of households headed by 35- to 44-year-olds, reports Martin Fleming, vice-president of Cahners Publishing Company in Newton, Massachusetts. Those ages bracket the nation's biggest spenders, especially on goods and services that are related to children and homes. Their numbers grow in the 1990s, but after 2000 they will embark on a long decline, "a phenomenon without historical precedent," Fleming said. In those years the advertising business will probably be softer than general growth. That's bad news not just for ad agencies but also for the consumer media that rely on advertising for support: magazines, TV networks, newspapers. More agencies will fail as America's rising numbers of giant companies turn to other giants to communicate their message. "There will always be national, regional, and local shops,"

Carl Spielvogel said, "but the large multinational ones are growing disproportionately."

This general consolidation raises serious issues of corporate governance. "Large corporate bureaucracies can be worse than government bureaucracies in losing sight of their customers," said S Jay Levy, chairman of the board of the Jerome Levy Economics Institute of Bard College. They catch "bigness disease," which resists new ideas, undermines internal financial controls, and engages in elaborate self-deceptions. Today's powerhouse combines are, by and large, being led by the most creative CEOs. Having bequeathed a behemoth to their successors, however, will they also leave a management structure that can tell itself the truth?

Think start-up

In an era of small net addition to demand, when most profits are wrung from shifts in the current business mix, nimble companies do the best. So there's a great future for start-ups and spinoffs that act quickly on new opportunities that arise. It takes whales to compete in the global economy. But the fattest profit margins may lie with the pilot fish that serve them and that snap up less conspicuous business along the way.

Befriend the trend

CEOs shape and reshape the international business landscape by macro-investing hundreds of billions of corporate dollars. After hours they micro-invest their personal money, and all these buster adjustments add up to some powerful stock-market trends.

Technology is the most pervasive, especially in capital equipment. To grow in the 1970s and '80s, businesses could afford to throw armies of workers into the breach. Trained labor was plentiful in those years; the excess supply helped slow the rise in the average wage. But to grow in the busted 1990s and beyond, business has to throw in capital. That favors cost-cutting equipment, especially in computers and communications. The most innovative technologies are typically found in smaller firms, and that helps explain the thrusting gains of small-company stocks.

Global integration, by contrast, favors large, energetic, and deep-pocketed companies, especially those with famous names. American consumers may be thinning out, but there's an explosion of purchasing power in the industrializing world, where American brand names stand for quality. Smart CEOs are finding

ways of buying in. The Gillette Company reports that 69 percent
of its revenues now come from abroad.

In America the wild card is how prosperous busters will become.
If, as predicted, they gradually do better than they expect, they'll
put less of a drag on the economy.

Right now, such hope seems slim. Fewer than 15 percent of the
people under 25 owned their apartments or houses in 1993, compared with 23 percent in 1973—and home ownership sets off the
economy's most productive chain of purchases. Still, some straws
in the wind suggest that that number could bottom out.

Houses have grown more affordable, thanks to moderating
prices and the decline in mortgage rates. For borrowers with a
fixed-rate loan, a starter home costs the same today, relative to
earnings, as it did in the early 1970s, when the ownership slide
began. A borrower with an adjustable-rate loan might be making
relative monthly payments as low as those in the 1950s.

Another measure of affordability is the number of new buyers
who live on a single income. Of those who earned $30,000 to
$40,000 in 1992, nearly 40 percent qualified for a mortgage on
just one paycheck, according to Chicago Title & Trust—a dramatic jump from 24 percent in 1991. That included the highest
percentage of never-married singles that Chicago Title had ever
seen.

It's also good news that some younger busters are marrying
earlier than most of the boomers did. If that develops into a trend,
it will speed up demand for apartments, condominiums, houses,
and all the purchases that go with them. The long decline in
household formation by people under 30 appears to have ended,
reports George S. Masnick of Harvard's Joint Center for Housing Studies.

To top off this hopeful news, the incomes of first-time home-
buyers are now going up relative to the cost of starter homes. If
this translates into higher rates of home ownership, the busters
will be giving more support to the economy by the year 2000 than
most analysts now expect. It won't resemble the buying binge of
the early 1980s, but it should develop into a market of modest
strength. That's the optimum buster world: modest, dependable,
persistent—and profitable—levels of growth.

TO ONE CITATION OWNER, THIS LOOKS LIKE PERFECT FLYING WEATHER.

When one University of North Dakota pilot sees a thunderhead like this, he flies directly into it. It's part of his job as a weather researcher. So far, his specially equipped Citation has carried him, his copilot, and a scientist right into the jaws of 600 severe thunderstorms. And right back out again.

It's good to know that Citations can survive rough weather, but it's better to know they don't have to. Citations are built to cruise at altitudes far above most storm clouds. And most weather researchers.

The Sensible Citations

Cessna
A Textron Company

Chapter Seven

POCKET MONEY: BRINGING BUYING POWER BACK

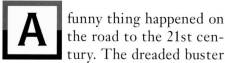funny thing happened on the road to the 21st century. The dreaded buster labor shortage never hit. In the early 1980s the gurus were warning that corporate growth was going to be throttled for want of young workers to meet demand. Yet today you might get 100 applications for a single opening. Spot labor shortages do arise for certain jobs or in certain regions. But those imbalances correct themselves as workers move and pay adjusts. Even though the recession officially ended in March 1991, America still is underemployed.

So CEOs have a different problem. Too few paychecks have left them with too few customers for the capacity they built up. Slower household formation means that new goods and services don't have to be produced as fast. Fewer workers are called for. So there's no labor shortage after all.

Furthermore, the supply of labor proved to be larger than anybody guessed. Expecting the worst, businesses imported skilled people, thanks to the eased immigration law passed in 1990. They redesigned jobs and invested in labor-saving technology to reduce the number of hires. They recruited the underemployed: women, seniors, minorities, and the disabled, all of whom rose to their new opportunities. They exported jobs to lower-wage countries where youthful workers are plentiful. The heightened inequality of income that developed during the 1980s put lower earners, including the young, well behind the traditional income curve. By the time of the 1990-91 recession, youths were especially vulnerable—occupying, as they do, the lower-wage slots that are being erased by technology, restructuring, and global competition. During that downturn, young people lost far more jobs than those in any other age group.

A case can be made that these melancholy trends will persist. Gary Shilling, for one, foresees no end to the current layoffs by bloated American businesses, no end to flat wages or purchasing power, and hence little hope that the young generation is going to prosper. He further doubts that many employers will go to the trouble of reengineering American jobs if it's easier and quicker to ship them offshore—and that includes white-collar jobs like computer programming and data processing. "There is excess labor worldwide today," Shilling said. "Americans are overpaid by global standards." Belonging to a small generation was a great help to workers in the 1950s, but—as he sees it—the magic won't work for the small generation of today.

In asserting that it will, I feel like the optimist who jumped off the top of the 30-story building and on her way past the seventh floor could be heard to shout, "So far, so good."

I start by asserting that in our dynamic economy the past is never prologue. Not only will the young raise their real wages, but during the 1990s those wages will rise at a faster pace than the earnings of the middle-aged, so that youths will truly improve their lot. The case for this view rests on five legs:

Better education. The busters show record-high levels of educational attainment. In 1990, when the latest data from the Census Bureau's Education Branch appeared, more than 40 percent of 18- to 24-year-olds had at least some higher education, including college degrees, compared with around 31 percent in 1980. On the low end, only 19 percent of today's 18- to 24-year-olds quit high school early, compared with nearly 24 percent in 1980. So more are in school and they're staying there longer. Furthermore, between 1987 and 1993, enrollment in community colleges rose three times faster than enrollment in four-year schools, and the biggest rise was among young people of traditional college age. It's in the community colleges that the modern technological work force is being trained.

All of this means that relatively more of the busters are fit for higher-paying jobs. As older (and less educated) workers retire, quit, or get promoted and their places are taken by younger people, the American work force becomes better trained. A higher education correlates with better lifetime incomes and lower unemployment rates.

So that's how the busters' story should end. Here at the beginning it's not so clear, because so many trained youngsters are having trouble finding work. One reason is that America now produces more college graduates than business needs, argues Gary Shilling. This sheepskin surplus pushes collegians into jobs that don't require so much training. It also undercuts their paycheck potential. On the other hand, when I got out of college my first full-time job was in *Newsweek*'s mail room (there being more educated women in those days than good jobs they were permitted to hold). Starting low means nothing as long as there is room to rise.

Will the busters find the room? America's best hope lies in high-value-added jobs that competing countries can't easily copy. The evolving global specialization looks something like this: (1) low-wage jobs go abroad, so (2) global standards of living rise, so (3) foreign consumers gain more purchasing power, so (4) they buy more sophisticated and technically based goods and services like telecommunications equipment, which (5) can be profitably produced in the United States, so (6) American employers scramble for well-trained workers and (7) raise their pay. Unfortunately we're not yet there. "You can take all the engineers on Route 128 around Boston [the region's high-tech strip] and they don't add up to the equivalent of one auto plant," Shilling said.

Nevertheless, rapid growth is expected in professional, administrative, and, especially, technical occupations. An old Rust Belt city like Akron, Ohio, is dotted today with small companies whose high-value technologies sell in both national and international markets. Those are the jobs that America's work force is training for and that will yield a higher real wage. Ten years from now, if trade barriers keep easing, such businesses could equal hundreds of auto plants. Technical workers have replaced the old blue-collar elite.

One other point: only 25 percent of today's economy is related to imports and exports. There's still a huge domestic sector that's relatively immune to international competition. "Many of those businesses, like hotels and restaurants, have lower-income jobs where wages have been dropping the most precipitously," said Labor Secretary Robert Reich. "To the extent there's a baby bust, there will be a smaller supply of workers and greater earnings for the people in those sheltered sectors."

During recessions or times of turtle growth, employers raise their hiring requirements—a shortcut to finding the very best workers in a surplus labor pool. As a city or region moves out of recession, however, and the labor surplus shrinks, companies lower requirements again. That's when higher-skilled workers start moving into better jobs and second-tier workers take their places, raising wages for both groups. You see this happening already in the fast-growing parts of the Middle West and the Southeast—greatly to busters' benefit. This trend will pick up as the states harder hit by the 1990-91 recession repair their economies and begin to move ahead.

Higher productivity. As part of America's vast business restructuring, whole layers of management and floorsful of white- and blue-collar workers have been taken out and shot. Many of them will never again find jobs at comparable pay. The cut in their purchasing power impedes the entire country's rate of growth. But this wholesale slaughter, cruel as it is, increases the productivity of the workers who survive. Productivity gains are also coming from two other CEO-driven tactics: the breakneck speed at which businesses are learning to use the microchip and the budding interest in job reengineering, which makes workers more valuable by raising their skills and responsibilities.

So far workers don't have much to show for the job losses and pay cuts they've sustained. Over the past decade manufacturing productivity has soared, but the added value went chiefly into profits rather than take-home pay. Although the labor-intensive service sector (82 percent of the work force) is just beginning its own drive for productivity gains, the improvements there also appear to be going to capital rather than to labor, said economist Irwin Kellner of the Chemical Bank.

Any new wave of technological change erases jobs—at least at first. And it's bad news that paychecks aren't keeping up with gains in productivity. The paradox of low pay is that while it can raise one company's profits, it lowers everyone's profits when all firms indulge. For a country to prosper, its workers have to be able to buy the goods they make.

But another lesson from American history is that new technologies ultimately increase employment, mostly in higher-value jobs. When that hiring hour finally arrives, the busters' small numbers will work in their favor, forcing companies to shift more of the productivity gains into workers' paychecks. When will this changeover occur? Best guess: in this decade's second half. Secretary Reich said that in manufacturing industries where skills count he already sees a greater willingness to retrain workers. "Because of the bust, employers have more incentive to train, which will make it easier to reduce a component of structural unemployment," he said.

Suitable skills. Confounding another set of pessimists, who see U.S. workers as underskilled, the abilities of most of the busters will be a good match for the jobs that business wants done. In any labor market some skills are in surplus while others are in shortage, but the great majority of workers are always sufficient to the task. A study published in 1990 by the National Center on Education and the Economy in Rochester, New York, found that 95 percent of employers do *not* expect their skill requirements to increase significantly (suggesting to me that CEOs aren't pushing change as fast as they could or should). When job requirements do change, "it's a gradual process," said Stephen L. Mangum, associate professor of management and human resources at Ohio State University in Columbus. "People and institutions adjust, as they're doing today."

On the higher end, jobs are being skilled up and so are the workers who desire them. Some states even custom-train production workers for companies that will locate there. Such training may not raise the pay of a middle-aged refugee from a Northern auto plant. But to a buster who so far has held only short McJobs, a high-tech production position is a clear step up.

On the lower end, jobs are being skilled down, so less-educated workers can touch a screen to tell computers to make critical production, inventory, and billing decisions. It's trickier to operate a forklift than to run some of today's computerized production lines. These jobs too can raise workers' productivity, but only as long as the job isn't dumbed down too far. A CEO can pursue a low-wage strategy by adding value to the machine rather than the operator, but the more explicit a robot's task, the more often it has to be upgraded. Simpler machines can be upgraded just by giving the operator new instructions, an approach that will probably be more productive in the end.

There is indeed a skills problem, but a narrow one. Some part of the youthful labor force is functionally illiterate or lacks the basic workplace know-how—on-time arrival, proper appearance, cheerful demeanor, willing attitude—that employers look for first. But to put this problem in perspective, "inadequate endowments have always been a problem for some portion of the potential work force," Mangum said. This is a formidable social problem but not a generational plight. Some of the missing skills, such as how to behave on the telephone, give and take direction, and treat customers right, can be taught by companies willing to invest in their employees. But correcting defective reading and writing skills, a scandal of the school system, is beyond the resources of employers.

A work ethic. Like the Depression generation, today's busters take jobs almost anywhere, spurred by a strong sense of economic insecurity. One sees résumés made up of gigs, not positions. The nomads of the work world, many busters move from company to company, project to project, always engaged in a short-term or part-time occupation. A young buster might clerk in a store for six months, sign on for office temporary work, then turn up doing polling for a research firm. They're the human equivalent of the just-in-time inventory-control system. As they stumble along, however, they're acquiring patience, experience, and skill. When they finally do land good full-time jobs, they'll perform with distinction, or at least determination. The busters put a high value on the chance to hang on to steady work.

The dynamic economy. No crisis lasts. The plant shutdowns will end; the excess global capacity will ease; the minidepressions on the East and West coasts will gradually clear up, probably toward the decade's end. Then businesses will expand again and the scramble for workers will finally begin. Even now you see some of the ways that the new economy will be raising pay:

• Boomer women are seeping out of the workplace (perhaps to raise children), and buster women are entering at a slower pace. This slows the growth of the labor force and improves the earnings outlook for those who remain on the job.

• America continues to attract skilled foreign labor—nurses from Ireland and the Philippines, engineers from India, England, and China—whose pay gives a lift to purchasing power.

• Rising standards of living in the newly industrializing countries will expand U.S. export industries, which are generally not low-wage.

• Public policy is promoting apprenticeship programs to bring more of the marginal young people into the overground economy. Some CEOs too are pushing diversity programs, which help raise wages for minorities.

• The burgeoning of small business today shows the great rewards of entrepreneurship—another way that creative workers can eventually raise their pay. Smaller enterprises, when they work, create equity that's rarely available in larger firms.

• Health care reform might end the dodge of employing cadres of part-timers just to avoid the insurance cost. The result could be fewer insecure gigs and a better shot at full-time work.

• As America ages, workplaces will increasingly be peopled by experienced employees, raising productivity even more. When those gains are finally passed along to workers, their pay can rise without pushing inflation up. Real purchasing power should begin to increase at a noticeably faster pace.

For years the baby boomers feared that they might be the first generation ever to be less successful than their parents. That worry came to naught. Studies done as recently as 1993, by both private and government economists, found that on average boomers boast substantially higher real incomes and net worth than their parents had at the same age.

Boomers gave up some family life to achieve their material goals. More wives went to work, including some who would rather have stayed home. More couples decided to have fewer children or none at all. But even adjusting for the number of paychecks and family size, boomers are outearning their parents' generation by sizable amounts, demographer Richard Easterlin reports. Even the boomers' savings rates are close to what their parents achieved and would probably be higher if the surveys counted saving through company retirement plans. Only low-earning boomers, especially from the younger age group, underperformed the low earners of their parents' years—reflecting the widening income gap between rich and poor.

Today it's the busters who fear they'll be left on the wrong side of that income gap. They're especially spooked by the drop in the real hourly wage that began in the early 1970s and continues to this day. But a far better measure is real wage and salary disbursements, which covers all employee pay and, except in recessions, generally goes up. It will rise for the busters too. The 1990s might not be a happy decade. But after that the baby busters might have it all—a living wage and more family life. For American business, no better outcome could be wished.

IN REAL LIFE, THE HARE BEATS THE TORTOISE EVERY TIME.

For years, the turboprop industry has claimed that slow and steady wins the race. To say that a turboprop is somehow more sensible than a jet is a harebrained notion at best. At nearly 100 mph faster, the Citation II outperforms turboprops in every category, at operating costs guaranteed to be lower. And for virtually the same purchase price.

Today, the turboprop story is little more than a fairy tale. And the time has come, once and for all, to close the book on it.

THE SENSIBLE CITATIONS

Cessna
A Textron Company

Chapter Eight

THE ENDGAME: ROLLING THE 21ST-CENTURY DICE

T his anxious decade shares much with the famous *fin de siècle* of 100 years ago, a previous age of low public confidence, high dudgeon, and widespread economic stress. Then, as now, longstanding political and social structures were coming apart under the pressure of mass immigration, fervent feminism, industrial consolidation, and huge disparities of wealth. Then, as now, new worlds stretched ahead on unmarked paths. Somewhere on those paths will arise the industries, great and small, that will reshape the early 21st century. To CEOs fall the duty, the privilege, and the thrill of dropping America's corporate bankroll onto the table and rolling the dice. Of all the eras that one could choose for being in charge of an enterprise, many would be easier than the 1990s, but few could be more pivotal.

The success of your business strategies cannot be predicted. But whatever you do, demographic melt will play a role. Throughout their lifetimes, the baby busters will stand between CEOs and their profit goals, constricting cash flows and forcing alternative investments. In these days of the busters' early youth, you are finding new markets by stepping over them (to young teens), through them (to boomers), and past them (to customers abroad). You are getting a little economic buzz from the Vietnam hump that is temporarily adding to the demand for cars and consumer goods. But it will be harder to find enough people to augment the busters' attenuated spending as they crowd into those home-buying years that matter so much to American growth.

In the previous chapter I argued that busters have a good shot at earning relatively more than the boomers did. Every CEO should hope that my thesis is on the mark. Their extra earnings wouldn't restore those exciting early-boomer times. But they'd buttress the hope of a profitable 3 percent economy, maybe running on for years. If, on the other hand, busters turn out to be underhired and underpaid, that growth target may be too high.

Here's where CEOs have a role not just in their company's bottom line but in the whole country's prosperity. As a global competitor you can be a low-wage, high-turnover producer, shipping jobs abroad and structuring the workplace for minimum-wage work here at home. Or you can be a value-added producer, redesigning the work flow to raise your employees' skills, productivity, and pay. The latter strategy tips your investments toward human capital, a company's most valuable resource in an information age. In passing, you also create more affluent consumers, who will help stir America's economic pot.

The second choice doesn't have to be made through the kindness of your bleeding heart (remember the story of the transplant patient who chose the heart of a CEO over that of a ballplayer because the CEO's was so little used?). High-value companies expect high profits and achieve them by combining low costs with good wages and high productivity. You'll find a first-rate discussion of these crucial issues in the 1990 book *America's Choice: High Skills or Low Wages!* from the National Center on Education and the Economy.

To push value-added training today is probably to talk to the wall, in the view of Irwin Kellner of the Chemical Bank. Corporations are still beguiled by downsizing—a craze, he says, that has taken on a life of its own. "These companies are like flocks of birds that follow the leader until the leader changes direction," Kellner grumbled. "The staffing up of the 1970s and 1980s went too far. Now they're overdoing the staffing down of the 1990s." Regrettably, downsizing will persist until some leading companies notice that they're losing business for want of an adequate staff. Once upsizing begins again, upskilling will be brought along.

And so will the busters, who stand to be the prime beneficiaries of the next rehiring cycle. Like the youth of the '50s, who saw their careers leap ahead in the 1960s and '70s, the youth of the '90s should emerge into their reward by the end of the decade or soon after. Then, unemployment should start a decline that will last for years, spirits will improve, and growth will advance—added to by growing demand from the baby boomlet coming up behind. A secondary engine will be the trailing baby boomers, last of their generation to marry, have kids, buy a home, and get a lawn to mow. Since I'm crystal-balling, I'll toss in an inter-generational deal cut by Congress with affluent boomer retirees, adjusting Social Security payments so that busters won't stag-ger under the bill. Everyone will be scrambling—boomer, buster, boomlet—to find a paycheck, to roll the dice. These will be excit-ing years.

In the course of researching this book, I spoke with many more CEOs than are quoted here. I didn't include them because the busters were off their screen. Some were focused on keeping up with the baby boomers. Some were absorbed in short-term prob-lems. Some gave no thought to demographic flux. The owner of a hugely successful direct-mail business hadn't even heard about buster decline but said, "You're telling me I should pay attention, right?" Right.

Every business should spend some time playing the buster game with the products and services it sells. What does the cohort shortage mean, not just today but in the future? When might your sales, or the sales of your best customers, fall behind? The auto industry, for example, might foresee a slide when the Viet-nam hump passes and the number of 25- and 26-year-olds declines again. The hotel industry might foresee a shortage of business travelers 10 years from now, when older executives get desk jobs and the buster generation hits the road. In light of analyses like these, what course corrections should you make? What news do you see in the trade papers whose meaning might be missed by those who don't grasp the power of demographic change and the coming hole in the market?

Whether your competitors see them or not, those tectonic plates keep on moving below your industry's bedrock assump-tions, shifting them toward some unexpected fault. The edge belongs to the CEO who not only sees their drift but *acts*.

PETER UEBERROTH SAW HIS NEW CITATION CABIN ON THIS SCREEN FOUR MONTHS BEFORE IT WAS ACTUALLY BUILT.

When entrepreneur Peter Ueberroth came to Cessna to select his new interior, we showed him hundreds of beautiful fabric and hardwood options. Moments later, we showed him something even better – a realistic simulation of his Citation cabin, with all his choices "installed."

This computer visualization system is just one of many surprising innovations at Cessna's new Customer Center. And it's one reason why our owners face no surprises at all when their Citations are completed.

THE SENSIBLE CITATIONS

Cessna
A Textron Company

ADDITIONAL COPIES

To order additional copies of *A Hole in the Market* for friends or colleagues, please write to The Chief Executive Press, Whittle Books, 333 Main St., Knoxville, Tenn. 37902. Please include the recipient's name, mailing address, and, where applicable, title, company name, and type of business.

For a single copy, please enclose a check for $13.95, plus $3.50 shipping and handling, payable to The Chief Executive Press. Discounts are available for orders of 10 or more books. If you wish to order by phone, call 800-284-1956.

Also available, at the same price, are the previous books from The Chief Executive Press:

Getting the Job Done
by Kenneth L. Adelman

What Are You Worth?: The New World of Executive Pay
by Graef S. Crystal

Pressure Points: The Phases of a CEO's Career
by Robert W. Lear

Found Money: Managing the Productivity Revolution
by Al Ehrbar

Who's in Charge?: CEOs and Boards Shuffle Power
by Richard M. Clurman

Getting the Talk Right: The CEO and the Media
by Robert Goldberg

The CEO Goes to Washington: Negotiating the Halls of Power
by Max Holland

Please allow two weeks for delivery.
Tennessee residents must add 8¼ percent sales tax.